# THE MISSING PEACE
*The Hidden Power
of Our Kinship with Animals*

Tina Volpe and Judy Carman

# THE MISSING PEACE
## The Hidden Power
## of Our Kinship with Animals

Dreamriver Press

Dreamriver Press LLC
www.dreamriverpress.com
or contact at:
12 Franklin Avenue
Flourtown, PA 19031-2006
U.S.A.

First Dreamriver Press edition, 2009

ISBN-13:  978-0-9797908-2-9
ISBN-10:  0-9797908-2-4

Library of Congress Control Number: 2009921516

1. NAT039000   NATURE / Animal Rights
2. OCC036000   BODY, MIND & SPIRIT / Spirituality / General


Designed by George D. Matthiopoulos


This book is printed on 100% recycled paper.

Printed and bound in Canada

## What people are saying about *The Missing Peace*

"*The Missing Peace* clearly shows, by example, how every individual counts and how much we really can do to reduce the pain, suffering, and death of the animals with whom we share earth, sky, and water—beings with whom we're supposed to coexist and not harm or kill for our own selfish reasons. This book is a wonderful collection of essays that show how smooth the journey for increasing our compassion footprint can be when we are mindful of how our actions influence the lives of other animals. Read this forward-looking book, read it again, make meaningful changes in your life, and share with everyone. Peace across species is truly possible and each of us holds the key for success. Never say never."

> **Marc Bekoff**, author of *The Emotional Lives of Animals, Animals at Play: Rules of the Game* and *Wild Justice: The Moral Lives of Animals* (with Jessica Pierce) and co-founder with Jane Goodall of Ethologists for the Ethical Treatment of Animals.

"This exceptionally moving, clear, passionate, yet balanced book will be an enormous inspiration to all those who believe, as I do, that our survival is dependent on the transformation of our understanding and treatment of animals. Harmony with all life is essential now to the survival of life itself, and this book is a must read for all those awakening to our responsibility to end our dominator vision and practice and to start to live in tender harmony with all things."

> **Andrew Harvey**, author of *Son of Man* and *The Direct Path* and architect of "Sacred Activism".

"If you are vegan, or considering becoming vegan, this book will help you find your way to a healthier life, one that does no harm to other sentient beings who love their lives every bit as much as you love yours. The stories will touch you the way they touched me."

> **Jeffrey Moussaieff Masson**, author of two *New York Times* bestselling books about the emotional lives of animals: *When Elephants Weep* and *Dogs Never Lie About Love*. His latest book is *The Face on Your Plate: The Truth About Food*.

"The book…is powerful and inspiring and affects me the same way *Peace to All Beings* did—acting like an inspirational self help book… In a world filled with suffering, particularly animal suffering, it's easy to become overwhelmed and cry out 'But what can I do?' The answer is *so much*, as presented in *The Missing Peace* in powerful and moving testimonies from people around the world making a difference by looking not only with eyes and brains, but with hearts filled with compassion and empathy. The great men and women who abolished slavery or fought for civil rights were ridiculed in their day just as the minority is today who say animals should not suffer for human pleasures. Contributors to *The Missing Peace* take on the accepted world-wide practice of animal exploitation and offer insights to deeper spiritual appreciation of the role of animals as they touch human lives. The stories in *The Missing Peace* are an inspiration to humanity to be our best selves."

    **Kay Pfaltz**, author of *Lauren's Story: An American Dog in Paris.*

"Many of us dream of a planet healed and nurtured by a universal reverence for life. Yet, until we begin to deeply grasp the power of our eating habits, we cannot bring this dream into reality. *The Missing Peace* is a book designed to help us make the dream come true—not only for the earth, animals, and people, but also for ourselves. We all want inner peace. This essential and fascinating book helps us understand with sudden clarity why that peace has been so elusive and shares with us the amazingly simple way to find it at last."

    **John Robbins**, author of *Healthy at 100*, *Diet for a New America*, *The Food Revolution*, *The Awakened Heart*, and *Reclaiming Our Health* and founder of EarthSave International.

"*The Missing Peace* does an extraordinary job of connecting the many aspects of animal exploitation and our complex relationship with animals. It is a beacon outlining the path to the Peaceable Kingdom, and as such, it bridges the gap between our aspirations and living in the world as it is today."

    **Jerry Simonelli**, attorney, former Representative in the Connecticut House, and animal activist.

"*The Missing Peace* is a gracefully written meditation on nonviolence toward all living beings. Combining wisdom from the great sages of the past and present with a set of marvelous personal essays, it inspires and guides the reader toward compassion for those who suffer most at our hands: the innocent animals whom we slaughter by the billions for food that we do not need to live long, healthy lives. A refreshing spring of spiritual wisdom, *The Missing Peace* will always be a treasured part of my library, kept close at hand so that I can drink often from its healing waters."

**Norm Phelps,** author of *The Dominion of Love: Animal Rights According to the Bible* and *The Great Compassion: Buddhism and Animal Rights.*

"*The Missing Peace* is a beautiful message of inspiration! It reveals the missing piece to the puzzle of human freedom and happiness. Over forty true-life stories poignantly reveal an empowering truth: that mindfulness and compassion toward animals is essential to our spiritual life. Our present crisis is a spiritual one, and this timely and timeless book lights the path to the higher consciousness required to solve our dilemmas. Read this book, share it, and discover the peace within that brings joy and freedom to our world."

**Dr. Will Tuttle,** Ph.D., composer, pianist, and former Zen monk, is author of *The World Peace Diet* and co-founder of Karuna Music & Art and the Prayer Circle for Animals.

# TABLE OF CONTENTS

# Acknowledgments

We are grateful to so many people that our gratitude would fill an entire book. Nevertheless, we'll do our best to keep it short so that we can all begin reading the great stories that follow. First of all, *The Missing Peace* would not exist without the hard work and generosity of the busy people who took the time to tell their personal and inspirational stories. Our endless and heartfelt thanks go out to each one of you.

We also wish to thank the wonderful folks who read parts or all of the manuscript at various stages and gave us helpful comments and contributions. Reverend Andrew Linzey, Jerry Simonelli, Norm Phelps, Jeffrey Masson, Gracia Fay and Robert Ellwood, Will and MadeleineTuttle, Andrew Harvey, Marc Bekoff, Kay Pfaltz, Keith Akers, and Beth and Daniel Redwood gave us valuable assistance and advice. We are also grateful for information, help and inspiration from John Robbins, Karen Davis, Holly Roberts, Lorri Houston (Bauston), Richard Schwartz, Eddie Lama, Christina Dicker, Gabriel Cousens, Rynn Berry, Doreen Virtue, Eckhart Tolle, Howard Lyman, Jim Mason, Father John Dear, Thich Nhat Hahn, Rita Reynolds, Ann Wilson, the many medical and environmental researchers who are proving the benefits of a nonviolent lifestyle, the late Virgil Butler and so many others.

Additional thanks go to Gracia Fay Ellwood of "The Peaceable Table", Kara Davis of Lantern Books, Karen Allanach of the Humane Society of the U.S.'s "Francis Files", and People for the Ethical Treatment of Animals for allowing us to re-tell some of the stories from their publications.

We extend our heartfelt thanks also to our editor, Richard Garvey-Williams, and our publisher, Theodore Poulis, who gave us their extraordinary patience, humor, and help as we journeyed through the editing and publishing process. Our endless gratitude also goes out to those who have inspired us over the years: the many great spiritual leaders and writers; the activists on the front lines rescuing and speaking out for the animals; our families and friends; and to our significant others, Tina's John and Judy's Michael, who helped with reading and

11

critiquing, as well as being lovingly patient with the many late nights and missed dinners while we sat at our computers.

Also, we thank you—our readers—for purchasing and sharing this book and helping the animals in so many ways. Most of all, we wish to thank the animals themselves. It is they who inspire us every day to find ways to represent them, to ask for mercy for them, and to pray for peace and freedom for them and for all beings.

> *Love all God's creation, the whole of it and every grain of sand. Love every leaf, every ray of God's light! Love the animals, love the plants, love everything. If you love everything, you will perceive the divine mystery in things. And once you have perceived it, you will begin to comprehend it ceaselessly more and more every day. And you will at last come to love the whole world with an abiding, universal love.*

Father Zossima
in *The Brothers Karamazov*
by Fyodor Dostoevsky

# INTRODUCTION

## Part I: True Stories of Finding Inner Peace

Through collecting the stories for *The Missing Peace* over the past couple of years, we have come across so many wonderful accounts of people who have changed their diets and noticed it led to a revolutionary change in their health, spirituality and level of compassion toward everyone and everything. These stories reveal there is a part of the human soul that appears to be numbed or hidden away when animals or their products are consumed. The compassion for all animals that exists within each of us is forced to remain dormant in order for us to consume, use or wear animals or their products—actions that defy our deeper nature to "do no harm". As Harold Brown stated when he recalled his past experiences as a cattle rancher, "It was like I had a light switch over my heart that I could turn on or off depending on who or what I was dealing with." Reverend Professor Andrew Linzey calls this affliction "spiritual blindness". When the sacred part of us is not liberated by eliminating all harm to any living being, it suppresses our compassion for others, and unfortunately, for the voiceless living beings who are not so fortunate to live on our planet.

Existing on a plant-based diet is a loving choice. It is a decision to refrain from contributing to harm caused to any living being. Imagine a life where caring for one another and sharing food, thoughts and love are the centerpiece of existence; one that involves laying your head on the pillow at night, knowing that today you caused no suffering.

Please join us as we share these amazing personal stories of people who have made some very simple changes in their lives and thereby made peace for themselves and, consequently, for many others. These changes are not only simple to do, they are also the very same actions taken by people of wisdom from ancient times to the present.

## Part II: Teachers of Health and Inner Peace

In Part II we find support for this promise of peace as we explore both ancient and modern teachings in Chapters Thirteen and Fourteen. A wealth of wisdom about how to be and how to give, and receive peace and joy has been shared for uncountable centuries. These teachers believed that it is essential for us to feel connected to all life instead of separated from it. They demonstrated that the reward for that sense of kinship is an all embracing joy and wonder.

Chapter Fifteen reveals the many benefits that can be realized by living on a plant-based diet. Among them is improved health, as well as the knowledge that we are significantly reducing harm to animals. By leaving animals off our plates, we help heal the environment, feed the world's hungry people, and contribute to world peace.

In Chapter Sixteen, we share our vision with you of what life on earth could look like with a unified ethic of kinship and reverence for all life. It would be a place of loving people who truly care about one another and the animals that share our earth.

In our Appendix, we offer a list of websites and books for continued study and a Frequently Asked Questions section. We will answer a few questions that may have arisen during the discussion of these issues.

This book was written to demonstrate how uncomplicated and rewarding it can be to transform to a kinder way of life—to embrace compassion for all living creatures and in return, flourish spiritually, in health and in heart.

> *You must be the change you wish to see in the world.*
> Mohandas K. Gandhi

# PART ONE

# True Stories of Finding Inner Peace

At the beginning of our research, we weren't sure how many stories we would find, but once we started asking people about their experiences, we soon realized there would be enough to fill several books. For example, Ricky Setticase, activist and animal shelter volunteer, asked himself the soul searching question "why [eat] these animals and not those?". Concluding that there was no answer for that question, Ricky gave up eating meat altogether. Following that transition and as his compassion continued to grow, he made a commitment to a nonviolent vegan lifestyle. So now, stated Ricky, "I buy products not tested on animals, I don't wear products from animals, and I am committed to educating the public about animal welfare issues. My motto is, 'to change one heart & one mind at a time'." This new path of compassion and what Ricky called a "conscious awareness of self and source" has brought him to, as he put it, "this moment in life where I feel truly connected".

Similarly, activist and author Lee Hall found that "From the moment I made the vegan commitment it became clear to me that I had been missing something. Something that touched the core of feminism, ecological activism, and the work to transcend prejudice and advance peace."

Since going vegetarian, author Denise Bennett noticed "changes on so many levels. As the body cleanses, so does the mind, freeing the spirit to explore and pursue higher ideals. Fear begins to fall away, leaving joy and inspiration in its wake." (1)

Maryanne Appel wrote that she would always be vegan, "and the lightness of spirit that this way of life gives me is exhilarating!" (2) Similarly, Duncan Myers stated that he finds [veganism] "very liberating...it's flat-out joy!" (3)

Erik Marcus, author and activist, has taught that, since switching to a plant-based diet improves our health, the resulting healing "sets the stage for a spiritual awakening..." (4) Time and time again we have seen such an awakening take place.

We will always be grateful to the people who have been willing to find the words to explain and celebrate their extraordinary spiritual transformations. May we all find inspiration in the stories that follow.

# CHAPTER ONE

# What Is Inner Peace?

*When the power of love overcomes
the love of power, the world will know peace.*
Jimi Hendrix

Inner peace is a feeling, a deep satisfaction of sorts—a realization that what we are doing in this lifetime is making this world a better place for others, human and non-human alike. When we are right with ourselves and the world, emotionally, physically and spiritually, everything and everyone that we come into contact with benefits. Our actions and reactions are more compassionate, our motives and the way we treat our brothers and sisters are kinder. We are no longer caught up in the struggle to accumulate things, but instead are more rewarded with the joy that comes from giving.

We can make the shift within ourselves, to find the love and compassion that is presently overshadowed by the noise and chaos of daily life. It has been said by many great people both in our world today and throughout history that when we love one another and all of creation, true happiness is found.

When I, Tina, interviewed a great author and friend, Reverend Professor Andrew Linzey on my radio show, he said that there is only one path to happiness, joy and inner peace. "It is to be of service." This approach releases the true and positive aspects of humanity within us. We are primitively programmed to be looking out for one another, being there when others are in distress. When love is shown through unselfish giving, we feel an incredible euphoria.

Reaching out with love is a path to peace, whether it is applied to human or non-human animals. If we are all interconnected through God and universal love, then every cruel act done to others, comes back to harm us. How can we exist happily when continuous harm to human and non-human animals is occurring? In a world full of truly loving and compassionate beings, everyone would be awake to the realization that we are all one.

So, the answer to the question of how to attain inner peace must be to love one another, including the plants, earth and animals, and never sway from that. Never take anything that has suffered into our bodies. The natural result will be a light coming on from within us. This will be the love light that will illuminate the path for others seeking their own light. This will be the light that shines for every living thing. And as a result, we discover that giving to others in need and showing love for all beings will become our life journey. Every effort we put forth to make another's life better, human or animal, will benefit our own spirit.

## Finding My Good Heart

*Beth Lily Redwood's quest to live by the ideal of lovingkindness led her and her husband to a shocking realization and a truth that beckoned her toward the life she wanted.*

A powerful dream of dying marked the beginning of my new life as a vegan. In the dream, I find out I'm going to die that day. I'm preparing my last will and an owl comes to guide me through my death. I try to lock the doors, but I can't, and a woman with a gun gets in. As I'm about to be shot, I choose to focus on the smiling face of the Dalai Lama; then I hear shots fired at me, and I wake up. A dream of transformation, of dying to an old way of life. A wise owl symbolizing higher wisdom to guide me, and the Dalai Lama, the incarnation of the Buddha of Compassion, as the energy with which I choose to align my consciousness, symbolized my dying to one level of awareness and awakening to another. The "last will" too is significant—in one sense, I directed my will to leave behind an old way of life to begin anew, and in another, it was a propitious, in-depth conversation with Will Tuttle, a 30-year vegan and author of *The World Peace Diet*, about the horrific suffering endured by farm animals to produce meat, dairy and eggs, that unlocked my compassion for these innocent beings and was key to my decision to become vegan.

There have been times in my life when synchronicity is so omnipresent that it seems as though God is winking. My fortuitous meeting with Will Tuttle was a true experience of "when the student is ready, the teacher will appear". My husband Daniel and I met Will and his artist wife, Madeleine, at a potluck at a friend's home in Virginia Beach, where we heard Will play transcendent, improvisational piano music, and we became interested in having him compose a "personalized music portrait" for each of us. That weekend, Will was speaking during the worship services, then giving a workshop on intuition at a Unity Church in Richmond. We'd have to go there to meet with him. I hesitated to go, since I was worried about a dear friend, Martha, a cancer survivor I'd helped in the past and who had not returned my phone calls asking about the latest results of her cancer tests.

But Daniel and I drove two hours to Richmond and arrived at the church in time for the second service, attended by fifty or so people, all strangers to me, and we sat in the front row. Early in the service, the minister paused for the congregation to "greet your neighbors", but talking to strangers made me uncomfortable and I turned toward my husband instead. Suddenly, a man I'd never seen before rushed over to me from the back of the room and said, "I just want to thank you for what you did for Martha." He then assured me that my dear friend's cancer tests had come out fine. What are the odds that Martha's former husband, who I'd never met, would be at this small, out-of-the-way church at this second service, having driven there from Virginia Beach with his girlfriend (a woman who recognized my husband), and that he would tell me exactly the information I needed for my peace of mind that day? I took this as a sign that I was exactly where I was meant to be. Little did I know that after that day, life as I knew it would never be the same.

Coming to church that day, I believed I was a person on a spiritual path, one highly influenced by Buddhist teachings on lovingkindness and compassion. I prayed daily "to be filled with lovingkindness" and for the happiness and freedom from suffering for "all sentient beings". I held the concept of "ahimsa", or non-harmfulness to any living being, as the basis for my spiritual path. I believed in the law of karma, or cause and effect—"As you sow, so shall you reap"—that whatever we do unto others will rebound to us. The Golden Rule of "do unto others as you would have them do unto you" was the guiding principle of my spiritual practice. I was part of a Gaian group that based their beliefs on the sacredness, oneness and interconnectedness of all life, and a women's group that honored the principle of the divine feminine. Seeing myself as a peace advocate, I volunteered countless hours for the Kerry presidential campaign hoping to help stop the war in Iraq. And above all, I considered myself "an animal lover", having adored cats most of my life and creating artwork honoring cats for a gallery's annual "cat's meow" art show.

Yet with all of these noble spiritual aspirations, I had failed to make the basic connection between my consumption of animal products and the painful, mortal consequences to the animal who was being consumed. Without realizing it, I was negating my efforts to be the kind of person I wanted to be—loving, compassionate, non-harmful, non-violent and peaceful—by engaging in the opposite behavior through my daily meal choices. In *The Tibetan Book of Living and Dying*, Sogyal Rinpoche explains, "Self-grasping and self-cherishing are seen, when you really look at them, to be the root of all harm to others and also of all harm to ourselves."

Music, art and meditation have the power to bypass our ordinary state of mind and transport us to deeper levels of awareness and intuition. Spending the day at the church, mesmerized by Will's uplifting piano music and Madeleine's radiant animal paintings, my deeper consciousness began to awaken. While Will composed music for my "personalized musical portrait", I felt myself transported to an inner dimension of consciousness where I connected with the soul of my being. In this peaceful, light-filled space, I experienced a kind of "life review" and glimpsed the meaning and trajectory of my life's path. Flooded with loving feelings, I intuited a higher purpose in my relationships, even those that had hurt me, and I saw birds and other animals who expressed gratitude to me for appreciating, feeding and sheltering them in my backyard "sanctuary". It was a transcendent experience in which I opened to a heartfelt sense of harmony and communion with all of life deep in the center of my being.

In *The Tibetan Book of Living and Dying*, Sogyal Rinpoche clearly describes my experience: "This (meditation) practice unveils and reveals your essential Good Heart, because it dissolves and removes the unkindness or the harm in you. Only when we have removed the harm in ourselves do we become truly useful to others. Through the practice, then, by slowly removing the unkindness and harm from ourselves, we allow our true Good Heart, the fundamental goodness and kindness that are our real nature, to shine out and become the warm climate in which our true being flowers."

That evening my husband and I shared our first conscious vegan meal with the Tuttles at a Chinese restaurant, and it was delicious. Prior to meeting Will and Madeleine, I had not known or even thought about what it meant to be vegan. Though I considered myself "mostly vegetarian", I regularly ate cheese and eggs, wanting to believe that dairy cows and egg-laying hens lived out their natural lives in an idyllic scene of farm life I'd seen in movies—enjoying sunshine, fresh air, healthy food and companionship. I was soon to learn how deluded I was about the reality of these animals' lives.

Though the information had been readily available, I had not learned about the experiences of farmed animals mostly because I was afraid it would be too upsetting. But the sad irony is that by walling myself off emotionally, I was perpetrating the very actions I found too disturbing to contemplate. In *The Great Compassion*, Norm Phelps writes, "Make no mistake, when you purchase a piece of meat, you are placing an order for an animal to be killed. You are responsible for the killing. The animal was killed for you."

The central premise of Will Tuttle's book, *The World Peace Diet*, is that there's a fundamental goodness in the heart of every person, but that we have severed the connection to our instinctive kindness by accepting the dominating cultural paradigm that eating animal foods is the way to be healthy and fulfilled. Furthermore, he believes that this disconnection from our wise heart and sense of connectedness with all of life is the root cause of the hatred, aggression, violence and suffering that human beings inflict on other living beings.

As Will explains, "Being unwilling and unable to see, confront, and take responsibility for the hidden ocean of horror that our most basic activity causes to those who are as sentient and vulnerable as we are, we have split ourselves into a schizophrenia of politeness and civility that lives uneasily with the remorseless cruelty that surfaces whenever we obtain or eat animal foods. I believe this split is the fundamental unrecognized wound we modern humans suffer, and from it many other wounds and divisions naturally and inevitably follow."

During dinner with the Tuttles, I began to get clarity about the treatment of animals raised for food, particularly the females whose eggs and dairy products I regularly enjoyed. Much to my horror

I learned that egg-laying hens and dairy cows endure some of the most severe suffering of all farmed animals.

Ever since college, I had found the thought of veal, a baby calf, to be utterly abhorrent, and I was appalled to learn that the dairy and veal industries were one and the same. The calf is produced because his mother must be impregnated and give birth to lactate the milk that nature intended for the baby. But that milk is subverted for human enjoyment, while the baby is forcibly taken away, kept in a dark, tiny stall chained at the neck, and fed a liquid, anemia-producing diet so he will have the soft, white flesh humans want to eat.

I was soon to learn a lot more about the unbearably sad and tortured lives of farmed animals. Saying good-bye to Will and Madeleine, I mentioned that the film *Peaceable Kingdom* was showing in Virginia Beach the following week, but that it sounded too disturbing to watch. Will simply said, "If the animals are going through it, I want to know what it is."

At that moment, I noticed how my ego wanted to shut down the deeper, awakening presence inside of me—my "good heart"—that was open to the truth of the consequences of my actions. On the one hand were my spiritual ideals of non-harmfulness, lovingkindness and compassion, of wanting to be a person of good will who acts in positive ways toward all other beings. On the other hand was what author Eckhart Tolle calls my egoic mind, the limiting, self-serving part of me that preferred the familiar comfort zone of habitual behavior regarding animals and my diet. If I was taking part in eating animal products, why was it so hard to look deeply at what that meant to the animals and what it might say about me as a person? But I took inspiration from Will's example of living in the wholeness and integrity that comes from making your actions consistent with the ideals of an awakened heart, and I found the courage to see the film.

As Eckhart Tolle explains in *A New Earth*, "Once you have had a glimpse of awareness or Presence, you know it firsthand. You can invite Presence into your life, that is to say, make space. With the grace of awakening comes responsibility. You can either try to go on as if nothing has happened, or you can see its significance and recognize the arising of awareness as the most important thing that can happen to you. Opening yourself to the emerging consciousness and bringing its light into this world then becomes the primary purpose of your life."

The following week Daniel and I attended a screening of *Peaceable Kingdom*, a deeply affecting documentary that shines a clear light on the brutal treatment of animals raised for food. In the factory farming system, the lives of these docile, sensitive, vegetarian animals are reduced to a cry of agony from birth 'til death. I cannot forget the look of abject terror on their faces, the sounds of their screams, bellows and cries, and the utter cruelty they were subjected to by the humans who electrically shocked, prodded, beat, dragged, hung them upside down, sliced their necks, and systematically killed them.

All of this unrelenting suffering of animals in the factory farming system is contrasted in the film with scenes from Farm Sanctuary, a paradisal safe haven for rescued farm animals. Here cows, calves, pigs, chickens, goats and sheep are seen living out their potential for happiness, pleasure, and affection with each other and with human friends. The film also features personal stories of former ranchers and the transformative experiences that led them to become vegans and animal rights advocates. I was especially touched by Harold Brown's story of how emotionally limited he'd been until Snickers, a deeply sensitive cow, put his head on Harold's chest and "turned on the switch" to the heart of compassion that he had shut down since childhood. [You can read Harold's story in Chapter Eight.]

As a woman and a mother, I identified with the intensity of the drive in animal mothers to love and nurture their babies. I was profoundly disturbed by the merciless exploitation and abuse of the females' bodies to obtain the maximum secretions (milk and eggs) before they are slaughtered at a prematurely young age for chicken pot pies, hamburgers and pet food once their spent bodies cease to be profitable. I cried as I watched a cow and her tiny calf be forcibly separated, then grieve for each other's company. And I was deeply moved by the plight of thousands of egg-laying hens who were the victims of a storm that destroyed their barn. While thousands were dumped alive into the trash, a few were rescued and the sight of them taking their first steps on solid ground in an atmosphere of love and kindness, was truly overwhelming.

For Daniel and me, *Peaceable Kingdom* removed the blinders from our eyes and catalyzed the opening of our hearts toward farm animals. The cruel, violent, horror-filled world of farmed animals we'd witnessed was not something that we as peaceful, compassionate, non-harmful people could stomach. When we left the screening, we went home and threw out everything in our kitchen that wasn't vegan. We thought we'd take thirty days to change our diet, because that's the amount of time we'd heard it takes to change a habit, but we both found that with what we now knew to be true, we could never go back to knowingly participating in any behavior that caused pain to an animal.

The next day we purchased an excellent vegan cookbook and found great local and online resources for everything vegan – from shoes and wallets to cheeses and vitamins. We educated ourselves about what it meant to be vegan. The word was created by Donald Watson in 1944, who defined it as follows: "Veganism denotes a philosophy and way of living which seeks to exclude, as far as is possible and practical, all forms of exploitation of, and cruelty to, animals for food, clothing, or any other purpose; and by extension promotes the development and use of animal-free alternatives for the benefit of humans, animals, and the environment."

We soon discovered that cruelty-free, vegan food was more flavorful and satisfying than anything we had eaten before. So many other people had gone before us in opening their eyes and hearts to animal suffering, and these people had laid the groundwork with wonderful resources for people to easily make the transition to vegan living.

In addition to meeting Will Tuttle and seeing *Peaceable Kingdom*, it was my lifelong love of cats that awakened my compassion for farm animals. There are currently three cats in my family, but my vegan lifestyle is the living legacy of one cat in particular, Lady Alfreda Butterfly Meow (named by my seven-year-old daughter). A delicate, graceful, green-eyed, calico beauty, with a deeply sensitive, empathic and protective nature, Alfreda was our beloved cat for just over seventeen years. Welcoming me home, delighting in my company, intuiting my emotional state, she loved me unconditionally.

When my husband and I wanted to see her, singing a few bars of "America the Beautiful" or "The Star-Spangled Banner" brought her bounding into the room. Daniel knew when I was about to arrive home by watching Alfreda position herself by the window. And she could always be counted on to stretch out on my lap or curl up by my feet on the bed at night, where she'd purr just from hearing me whisper, "I love you, Alfreda."

When Alfreda became ill from hyperthyroidism, her pain, frustration, and longing to remain part of socializing with the family she loved, awakened a deep recognition within me of how much we were alike. Though we were from different species, more than anything we both wished for happiness and freedom from pain. In short, we shared "sentience", the capability of experiencing pleasure and pain through the senses.

Through connecting with Alfreda so deeply, I began to realize what speciesism (the prejudiced belief that humans are superior to other species) had prevented me from seeing—that billions of farmed animals, whose bodies and byproducts are eaten and used by humans every year, are individuals in their own right, with distinct personalities and lives that are meaningful to them.

Philosopher Jeremy Bentham explains that it is the sentience we share with nonhuman animals, rather than the differences in our modes of rational thought that is the key factor in determining how we should treat them. As he stated, "[A] full-grown horse or dog, is beyond comparison a more rational, as well as a more conversible animal than an infant of a day, or a week, or even a month, old. But suppose the case were otherwise, what would it avail? The question is not, Can they *reason?* Nor, Can they *talk?* But, Can they *suffer?*"

Witnessing Alfreda's pain, I realized that what hurt her would hurt me too because we shared the same nervous system. As Will Tuttle explains, "We know today that all vertebrate animals are endowed with central nervous systems with proprioceptors that are sensitive to a variety of painful stimuli, including being cut, burned, crushed, confined, electrically shocked, and subjected to cold and heat, noxious smells, bruising, and chafing, and that they feel psychological pain as we would when they are physically confined, their babies are stolen from them, or their innate drives are systematically thwarted."

Albert Einstein challenged us to open our hearts to our fellow beings, both human and nonhuman: "A human being is part of the whole called by us the 'Universe', a part limited in time and space. We experience ourselves, our thoughts and feelings as something separate from the rest. A kind of optical delusion of consciousness. This delusion is a kind of prison for us, restricting us to our personal desires and to affection for a few persons nearest to us. Our task must be to free ourselves from the prison by widening our circle of compassion to embrace all living creatures and the whole of nature in its beauty."

On the morning of July 30, 2005, as I comforted and cradled my beloved Alfreda in my arms, she suddenly made a movement as though she was leaping toward some unseen being, and she left her body. The love and tenderness I felt for Alfreda, the fullness of her individuality, how lovingly she responded to my love, and my understanding of how we shared the same essence, became my model for seeing the sacred wholeness in all animals. For that gift of awakening my "good heart", I am forever grateful to my beloved Alfreda.

For as long as I could remember, I had considered myself "an animal lover", but now I understood that I'd only been a cat and dog lover. As Jane Goodall states, "Thousands of people who say they 'love' animals sit down once or twice a day to enjoy the flesh of creatures who have been utterly deprived of everything that could make their lives worth living and who endured the awful suffering and the terror of the abattoirs—and the journey to get there—before finally leaving their miserable world, only too often after a painful death."

Feeling an awakened appreciation for farm animals, I was enthusiastic about meeting them face to face for the first time. An invitation to 'Thanksgiving WITH the turkeys and their friends' seemed like the perfect way to celebrate this sacred day of gratitude for the blessings of life, with a cruelty-free feast that all beings could enjoy. The highlight of the day was watching turkeys and other birds happily devour a giant green cabbage. The sponsor of this event, United Poultry Concerns, is a sanctuary in Virginia, dedicated to "the compassionate and respectful treatment of domestic fowl", which includes turkeys, hens, roosters, ducks, and geese. The fortunate few who are rescued from the fate that awaits over 30 billion such birds every year, spread their wings, walk on the ground in the fresh air, and engage in natural behaviors. Daniel and I found these graceful beings to be full of curiosity, friendliness, individual personalities and a zest for life.

A few weeks later, Daniel and I met the residents at Poplar Springs Animal Sanctuary, a 400-acre refuge for farm animals and wildlife in Maryland. We petted pigs who seemed to smile from ear to ear, a curious turkey who looked you right in the eye, goats and sheep who ran in childlike abandon over open pastures, and cows with their beautiful, innocent eyes relaxing in the sunshine. Despite the happiness these animals were experiencing, it was sad to see the physical deformities and lifelong pain they endured as a result of the factory farming practices that mutilated and forced their bodies to grow so rapidly that their organs and legs struggled to support them.

The sanctuary reminded us of *Peaceable Kingdom*'s Farm Sanctuary and farmer Brown's story of how Snickers the cow turned on the switch to his heart, so he decided to sponsor her. Daniel and I considered which animals we owed the largest karmic debt to, and he chose to become a monthly sponsor of a turkey, while I chose a cow.

It was a blessing to be in the presence of farm animals and to hold in my heart only good intentions for their happiness. I felt a sacred kinship with them as fellow beings created by a loving God. I understood that God's peaceful kingdom will only come about when humans recognize that our dominion over animals is an instruction to act as kind stewards of their well-being.

Will Tuttle speaks about the sacred lives of all beings: "We are all expressions of the infinite creative mystery force that births and sustains the universes of manifestation, and our bodies and minds are sacred, as are the bodies and minds of all creatures. Like us, animals have feelings and yearnings; they nest, mate, hunger, and are the conscious subjects of their lives. They make every effort, as we do, to avoid pain and death and to do what brings them happiness and fulfillment."

One of my favorite passages from the *Dhammapada*, a collection of the Buddha's sayings, expresses my beliefs:

> All beings tremble before danger, all fear death.
> When a man considers this, he does not kill or cause to kill.
> All beings fear before danger, life is dear to all.
> When a man considers this, he does not kill or cause to kill.
> He who for the sake of happiness hurts others
> who also want happiness, shall not hereafter find happiness.
> He who for the sake of happiness does not hurt others
> who also want happiness,
> shall hereafter find happiness.

I was fortunate to have experiences that showed me the truth of animal suffering and lifted the veil that separated me from my compassionate heart. For many years, I've heard about the coming of a time when our world will be transformed into a place of love, light, peace and good will to all beings. I believe that in order to create this new world, the prerequisite missing piece is to connect to the soul of our being, to our inner wisdom that embraces the sacred oneness of all life. We cannot say we want to live in peace, then ignore the violence on our plates. We cannot absolve our complicity in harming innocent beings by saying prayers of gratitude as we eat the products of their suffering. Becoming vegan is a first step in walking our talk—a catalyst toward awakening the higher consciousness that will make our vision a reality.

Over centuries of history, there were times when human sacrifice, slavery, child labor, the oppression of women, apartheid, and segregation enjoyed broad acceptance. Virtually everyone in the Western world now sees these as appalling examples of fundamental injustice, yet at the time a few clear-sighted individuals took a moral stand and became catalysts for change. Margaret Mead said it best: "Never doubt that a small group of thoughtful, committed citizens can change the world. Indeed, it is the only thing that ever has."

I believe that someday we will look back upon the abuse, killing, and eating of animals with the same horror as we now view the most egregious injustices in history. In *The Animal Kingdom: A Spiritual Perspective*, the Ageless Wisdom teachings predict: "The time will come, when the attitude of man to the animal kingdom will be revolutionized, and the slaughter, ill-treatment, and that form of cruelty called 'sport', will be done away with."

We don't need animal foods in order to live or be healthy. In fact, research has clearly shown that animal foods are among the leading causes of the major diseases of our times. But most of us have been so strongly influenced by cultural traditions toward eating animals that we are unconscious of the deeper spiritual implications of our behavior.

The choice to become vegan may seem to some people an inconsequential act given the ocean of suffering in the world today. While there is little or nothing we can do to make a difference in most other situations, with animal suffering, our food choices directly contribute to more or less suffering. The suffering of animals is local and also intimate—their flesh and secretions (milk and eggs) are incorporated into our own bodies—they then literally become us. The eating of animals is among the most intimate relationships imaginable. Just as we would not want other intimate relationships in our lives to be contaminated with suffering and oppression, why should our relationship to animal foods be any different? Gandhi taught us to "Be the change you wish to see in the world." By not ingesting animal foods, I am free from their ill effects, but more significantly, I am not absorbing the energy of the pain, terror, hatred and sorrow with which the animals met their deaths.

A while ago I was having lunch with a colleague when a waiter walked by with a tray of animal foods, and she asked, "Aren't you ever tempted?" Without hesitation, I answered, "No, instead of seeing something appetizing, I see the being on the plate." In truth, it's the opposite of temptation. Without the "glamorizing" filter of advertising and cultural conditioning, I see animal foods as the mutilated, decaying corpses of traumatized, sensitive fellow beings. And my heart goes out to them.

People often think that being vegan is difficult or unnatural, yet I've found it to be the joyful, natural unfolding of the awakening of my "good heart". A couple of years ago *VegNews* magazine had a contest that asked for three words that best described your experience of being vegan. "Love over lust" were the words I submitted that won first prize.

Every spiritual value I hold dear has been enhanced through the daily, mindful practice of choosing compassionate, cruelty-free meals. Veganism honors the heart of the divine feminine because it extends tender loving care toward all beings. It respects the dignity of the bond between a mother and her child, and abstains from harming that child or ingesting products obtained from exploiting and abusing the female body. Compassionate consumption is the manifestation of Gaian consciousness, in that a plant-based diet is the most powerful step we can take toward caring for the planet, decreasing global warming and increasing the resources to feed the world's hungry people. It is the alignment of my personal will with a vision of a world of light, love, peace, harmony and unity, in which all life is revered and embraced with lovingkindness.

Being vegan is an everyday blessing. It's a gift that I seemingly give to animals, yet it gives back to me a hundredfold. The Bible says, "As you sow, so shall you reap," and as I extend peace, love, and goodwill toward others, those qualities return to me. The practice of veganism is the everyday blessing of the joy of expressing a loving heart, the wholeness of making my actions consistent with my beliefs, the peace of living in harmony with all beings. My energy feels lighter, brighter, and I'm more aware of my oneness with the beauty and blessings of life. It's as though something that had been broken is now healed and I've awakened to a new life—a life in which I've come home to my true self.

© *2008 Beth Lily Redwood*

## Karmic Debt

*Alice Williams explains in her story how her desire to live a spiritual life and keep her mind "in a higher place" led her ultimately to becoming a vegeterian.*

Well, I was convinced that a vegetarian diet was healthful, tasty, and environmentally friendly. However, convincing my son Lee was another matter. I ended up preparing two types of meals, and as a single working mom and also a student in college, well it was a bit much. So that time the experiment didn't last very long. But I imagine the seeds that were planted during my first foray into vegetarianism took root more deeply than I realized at the time.

About five years later I made some new friends who were vegetarian for different reasons. This time there was a strong spiritual component to the choice of not eating meat. I admit that in the 1970s I hadn't thought that much about moral arguments for being vegetarian. But now I had a new perspective on other consequences of what was involved. I was introduced to the idea of karma, and the belief that the slaughter of animal life meant taking on karmic debt. While it is true that vegetables are alive, too, and you have to kill them to eat, the understanding is that it is the least harmful to eat vegetables. There is a greater karmic burden from eating meat. Being vegetarian was part of the choice to lead a moral life, to refrain from harming other living things, and to seek to keep one's mind in a higher place.

I made a lifestyle decision to be vegetarian in 1981, and with my earlier experiences, it wasn't a difficult decision to make at all. I discovered new cookbooks—*Laurel's Kitchen, The Moosewood Cookbook, Changing,* and others. Tofu was readily available in most grocery stores, and new soy products had been introduced, making the change away from a diet that included meat quite easy. It was no longer considered unhealthful, and information about nutrients that needed to be included in a vegetarian diet and how to obtain them was easy to find. Putting the spiritual decision into practice was easily supported, especially here in southern California...

For me, being vegetarian now is most importantly part of being on a path to God. It supports my spiritual journey, and is supported by the spiritual view of life. It's a path I am happy to be on.

*Williams, Alice. Online Vegetarian Friends journal*
*"The Peaceable Table", April, 2005, vegetarianfriends.net.*

## The Golden Rule

*Here Peter Hartgens shares the story of his long journey to a life of compassion and inner peace and how what he eats and uses is such an important part of the treasure he has found.*

Since childhood I have heard the urging of the Inner Voice to live non-violently and to seek the ways of understanding, peace and harmony—basically, simply to live the Golden Rule.

My parents practiced no particular organized religion, and, overall, taught living the Golden Rule as the main instrument of "salvation". To them good deeds provided upliftment. As I grew up I studied different religions. It became apparent to me that the Eastern religions tended to promote vegetarianism and veganism, claiming that such fare respected the sacredness of life by not spilling the blood of animals for food, and, secondly, because vegetable food as one's source of nutrition calmed people, made for more harmonious digestion, and thus fostered peace and calm for deeper meditation.

Even in Western religion I found this leaning to vegetarianism. For example, I came to understand that among the prophets in the Hebrew Scriptures, Daniel and his companions in exile partook only of vegetable food to express their loyalty to Israel's God. My inner being exclaimed that such ways were true and right.

But I was rebellious. Simply, I liked excitement, and animal food aroused more internal excitement. And although my parents attempted a balanced omnivorous diet, I for the most part was a meat eater. I did eat fruit once in a while, but no more vegetables than

I could help; the only ones I consumed on any regular basis were french fries and onion rings on hamburgers. Also I ate a lot of cheese on hills of pasta. But the main item on my menu was flesh, very rare, and sometimes raw.

During this period I had colds and flu more of the time than I was healthy. Although I did not realize it at the time, I was also lactose-intolerant.

Though I went out of my way to avoid violence to other humans, I was destructive to myself: besides the harm I caused myself by flesh and dairy consumption, I was a substance-abuser (alcohol, illegal drugs) from age 11 to about age 30. After my marriage had failed, I fell deeper into patterns of self-destruction.

Finally I declared to the Creator that I was willing to turn my life around for my sake and my children's sake. More light came to me, including information on the restorative power of vegetables on bodies ravaged by substance abuse. Initially I went on a vegetable and fruit regime to cleanse myself. After a time I fell to meat-eating again, but since I was continuing with the vegetable food as well, I was healthier. The alcohol and drugs became a thing of the past.

However, my Inner Voice urged me to live more fully the Golden Rule, and that, the Light made clear, meant not eating animals. It became a struggle between my lower self and my spiritual nature.

I was confused about the health issue; I had heard for years that people need animal protein, and I had worries about my health, but the East Indian material I had encountered said plainly that we not only do not need it, we would all be healthier as vegetarians or vegans. So I set about studying the matter more closely. In the process of this search I came across a book called *Oahspe*. It claims that throughout history there have always been groups of people who worshipped an everpresent Creator, ate vegetable food, and would rather suffer death than take the life of another. It also asserted that a vegetable diet would be a help in developing the prophetic state (which I have not yet attained). For me, the book provided the first nail in the coffin of flesh-eating. I stopped for good.

When I was on a meat diet, even though I engaged in meditation and prayer, I had a volcanic temper. Since I have become a vegetarian, and now a near-vegan, I have found that I have greater peace; the volcano has not erupted in over fifteen years. I have also found that I am more open to subtler vibrations; spiritual perceptions are clearer. Simply put, I find it much easier to be in the world but not of the world. And not only am I free of the bloodlust, I have no desire for drugs or alcohol (though I still have a caffeine problem that I'm working on).

Human beings, for me, are assigned to be the caretakers of the world—an assignment we have nearly blown. Our non-human brothers and sisters are to be attended to and learned from, not dismissed as things; cared for, not tormented and butchered. Only then can we find peace within ourselves and with one another.

*Hartgens, Peter. Online Vegetarian Friends journal*
*"The Peaceable Table", June, 2005, vegetarianfriends.net.*


## Products of Slavery

*Here Gracia Fay Ellwood, the editor of the "Peaceable Table", shares the spiritual and emotional benefits that she has gained from drawing open the curtains that so many keep closed to hide the suffering of animals. By ending her own inner numbness in this way, she has found the joy that compassion in action brings.*

I grew up on a farm in Washington State in the 1940s and '50s, eating a meat-and-potatoes dinner 365 days a year. I loved my cats and found baby chicks and goslings and calves very appealing; the idea of animals being killed for food made me uncomfortable occasionally, but since I didn't have to do it or see it done, I tried, pretty successfully, not to think about it. Vegetarianism would never have been an option in our family. I first heard of it in grade school from a children's biography of Louisa May Alcott; despite my kindly heart, vegetarianism just seemed an oddity, though Louisa May seemed to have a lot going for her in other respects.

I first tried going meatless for Lent in 1971, by which time I had given the matter more thought and was wanting to live consistently. I enjoyed all the new dishes, but my husband, though he also liked them, unfortunately found himself getting more and more debilitated. We put this down to his need for more protein, and after Easter went back to flesh-eating. Later, when we had a baby, medical people told us we would be depriving him of necessary nourishment if we didn't feed him meat, so that was that.

It wasn't until the early 1980s, by which time we had begun to associate with Theosophists, that we started to reconsider the matter. We went to a vegetarian Theosophical camp every year, and found the food was good. I had heard that people on a vegetarian diet were more open psychically and spiritually, which sounded very appealing to me. I dropped meat after the 1985 camp and scarcely missed it. I also stopped serving it to my family. This time my husband did not get debilitated; apparently it was a matter of mind rather than protein.

The change in diet did not noticeably help me focus my mind in prayer and meditation, or give me any psychic experiences, but the new regime seemed right and I continued. In the early 1980s I had become a Quaker, and having committed myself to nonviolence, I soon followed the diet chiefly for reasons of compassion for my fellow animals.

By the 1990s I had become aware that so-called "food animals" suffered not only in slaughterhouses but also in agribusiness dairies and chicken farms, both better termed concentration camps for animals. I had also learned that these supposedly healthy foods were actually doing us more harm than good. But to my dismay I found that cheese and ice cream were a lot more difficult to stop eating than meat had been. In about 1996 at a religious studies conference I participated in a discussion dealing with slavery. Something clicked. I had to face the fact that agribusiness dairy and eggs were products of slavery, particularly cruel forms of slavery at that, and I knew I simply could not finance such systems any more. Words, I find, matter. Soy ice cream, incidentally, I now enjoy just as much as the other kind; cheese I dropped, and no longer miss.

These reasons for abstaining from animal products mostly had to do with animal suffering and human illness, unpleasant matters that many people, including many fellow [Quaker] Friends, did not want to hear about. And, of course, the prospect of such a diet seemed very depriving to them. After years of distress over this resistance, in the last month or two I have begun to realize that the other side of compassion, or "suffering-with", is joy. Closing one's heart and mind to the vast pain underlying the animal-food industries results in a state of numbness toward them that most folk take for granted. But numbness not only shields us from pain, it also cuts us off from delight. Many activists have found that actually meeting "farm animals" living in a more natural condition is a source of intense joy. We have come to see that pigs and cows not only love their babies in obvious ways, they also show love for and gratitude to their human caretakers. Though I have not yet really visited a farm since I lived on one, I relate strongly to these stories and to accounts of animals' capacity for fellow-feeling and altruism. They are not, after all, so different from my beloved cats, except perhaps in not being quite so cuddly.

I am coming alive as I explore more and more deeply my commitment to ahimsa at the table.

*Ellwood, Gracia Fay. Online Vegetarian Friends journal*
*"The Peaceable Table", November, 2004, vegetarianfriends.net.*

# CHAPTER TWO

# Opening the Heart to Compassion

*What is a loving heart? It is a heart that burns with love for all creatures...all created things...Immeasurable pity wrings the heart... It can no longer endure even the slightest pain inflicted on a created being...It prays even for the snakes, moved by the infinite compassion which is awakened in the hearts of those who are becoming like God.*
Isaac the Syrian

The stories people have shared with us in this chapter bring home an ancient truth. Great teachers have taught this to humanity for many centuries, but only a rare few individuals have grasped its deep and profound meaning—that is, until now. It is in this time of planetary awakening that people from all walks of life are receiving, acting on, and benefiting from this great wisdom. What is this earth-shaking message? It is simply this—we will find inner peace, and the world will see an end to violence only when we share our compassion and peace with all others. The key word is "all". Sharing loving kindness and peace only with our fellow humans is not enough to bring the heaven within for which we long.

When our hearts open to all species, to all beings, we will find the peace that eludes us—the missing peace. Albert Schweitzer once said, "Until we extend our circle of compassion to include all living things, we will not ourselves find peace."

The world-view that we must dominate and exploit nature, animals and other human beings permeates nearly every culture on earth. The endless wars, environmental devastation, species extinctions, slavery, etc. that fill our human history are ample testimony to that. We can not survive as a species with such a world-view, because we will destroy all that sustains us physically.

And while this outmoded paradigm threatens our physical survival, it also causes great spiritual anguish. Domination thrives on violence, and wounds all of us and all of life both physically and spiritually.

The good news is that the new world-view of cooperation and mutual respect for all earthlings and all of nature is blossoming. There are stories surfacing around the world of people creating new cultures, new communities of peace. This massive paradigm shift is indeed happening. There truly is hope.

The stories you are about to read are examples of the profound awakening that occurs when we open our hearts to compassion for all species—no matter how small, no matter how exploited, no matter how seemingly insignificant their lives appear to be to the current culture.

## From "Skinny Bitch" to *Skinny Bitch*

*Author of* New York Times *bestseller* Skinny Bitch, *Rory Freedman, a former agent for Ford Models, describes herself as a "self-taught know-it-all". Her co-author, Kim Barnouin, is a former model who holds a Masters of Science degree in Holistic Nutrition. They have successfully counseled models, actors, athletes, and other professionals using the "Skinny Bitch" method. They both live in Los Angeles.*

I don't know why or when it started, I only know that for many years, I was somewhat miserable. There was nothing wrong in my life—nothing bad. I was just unhappy, unfulfilled, and negative. Of course I had moments of goodness, but overall, my state of being was one of angst.

The one thing that always soothed me, however, and made me feel happy, fulfilled, and positive, was spending time with animals. I was the biggest "animal lover" I knew—I even thought I might be a veterinarian some day. But surprisingly, in all my years of being an "animal lover", I ate meat and chicken and eggs and dairy products seven days a week. I never considered how cows, pigs, and chickens went from living, feeling animals to food. But then one day, I got a magazine in the mail that had an article about factory farming and slaughterhouses. Until then, I avoided thinking about how animals were raised and killed so I could eat them. If the thought did enter my mind, I'd quickly imagine Old MacDonald's idyllic farm with happy animals and green pastures. I couldn't have been more deluded. What I learned from that magazine that day was shocking, devastating, and painful.

I decided then and there that I would never eat an animal ever again. And I can honestly say, it was the best decision I've ever made in my entire life. It was a choice I made for the animals, but what I got back in return was a life I didn't even dare to dream of. In the blink of an eye, I went from "me, me, me" to "I don't care about my own selfish desire to eat meat; I will never contribute to the slaughter of animals ever again." It was the first time in my life I understood that being of service was endlessly more satisfying than getting, getting, getting.

Becoming vegetarian, and eventually vegan, showed me a world of kindness, compassion, and selflessness. I became the kind of person I could be proud of—someone who cares about animals, people, and the planet. Where before, I wanted to be the best person, I now wanted to just be a good person.

It's been fifteen years since I made the decision to stop eating animals. And as a result, I am an entirely different being from that angst-filled, selfish, adolescent I once was. Don't get me wrong, I'm far from perfect. But every day, I can look myself in the mirror and know that at the very least, I'm doing right by the animals. And today, that's all I need to feel happy, fulfilled, and positive.

## After Loving a Pig

*Carrie Snider's deep love for animals led her to a heartfelt prayer for comfort. The gift she received from that prayer has blessed her ever since.*

I was an animal-lover long before I was a believer. As a young child, I dreamed of being a vet, a marine biologist, an animal trainer—anything to get me around animals. I gave up eating animals at age four, and I gave up milk and eggs (because of the way cows and chickens are treated in the farming industry) at age twenty. But it's my faith that brings me to animals in a soul-binding way. I now respect animals in a way that is neither patronizing nor exploitive, and I have my faith largely to thank...

After working at a farm sanctuary for a year, I became very close to a special group of pigs. They lounge in the sun happily, run to greet me when I bring them avocado sandwiches or lettuce hearts. They are pure joy.

Of all the animals on the sanctuary, it is the pigs who have brought into my awareness how unconscionable it is to mistreat farm animals. After loving a pig, one can never sit down and eat one.

My joy that comes from the pigs often turns to pain. I venture out of my sanctuary bubble and encounter the dead remains of mistreated animals, including pigs, everywhere. It hurts, as it did at age four, when my mother told me the truth of where meat "comes from". It hurts to know that animals are killed merely for their taste and often in gruesome ways, with no thought to the kind of beings they are.

One night, emotions boiled over and I surrendered to tears. "Do You have a place for the animals?" I asked God. "Do You want more for them?"

As I continued a long, rambling prayer, asking for comfort, I was interrupted by a steady, quiet inner voice: "Let the children come to me," it said. I immediately saw an image: Jesus, arms outstretched, awaiting his children. Birds flew to his arms, geese waddled to his feet, and pigs lumbered up the hill, slowly yet joyfully. It was then that I realized: these animals are just the sort of beings God begs us to be: joyful; accepting; forgiving; trusting; waiting, excited for the next surprise.

Now, whenever I become overburdened with the horror imposed on farm animals, I remember those words, that image, and the happy piglets. They are (I can't doubt it!) among God's chosen people.

*Snider, Carrie. Humane Society of the United States "Francis Files". The website is hsus.org/religion.*

## Lessons from a Giant Lobster

*Amy Hughes is a yoga teacher in London. Many yoga teachers, like Amy, eat only a plant-based diet and live by the principle of ahimsa (the Sanskrit word for harmlessness, nonviolence, and unconditional love). It enhances their yoga practice, increases an inner sense of well-being and peace, and above all is consistent with the very values of yoga itself. In her story you will read how some startling and unsettling discoveries led Amy to an ancient promise.*

At the age of seventeen, I became a vegetarian. I can recall the moment it happened. I was out with my boyfriend Patrick at the time. He took me to a Japanese restaurant where you sit at large family style tables with other people, and the chefs prepare and cook your meal at your table. We ordered steak and shrimp. When I saw the raw meat being wheeled out on the trolley, my stomach turned. I didn't see food that I was eager to eat; I saw dead animals. I didn't want to spoil the evening, so I ate the meal we ordered, but that was the very last time I ate meat. And it was not at all difficult. However, I continued to eat fish. So truly, I was not yet a vegetarian.

Nearly ten years later, I was camping in Maine with my boyfriend at the time, Bela. One night, we bought live lobsters to eat for dinner. Growing up, lobster dinner was always a very special treat. We would buy live lobsters, bring them home and cook them in boiling water. I would watch as my parents dropped these living animals in the pot, feeling sorry for them, often observing that as they were submerged in the boiling water, they would raise their claws as if in a last desperate plea for help. But I thought they tasted good and didn't feel bad eating them. However, on this occasion it was very different. Bela explained to me one anatomical feature of a lobster, which is an exoskeleton. I had never heard the term, and it made me realize that a lobster is a living creature whose skeleton is on the outside and whose flesh is on the inside. How extraordinary! Again, I did not want to spoil the evening, so I ate the lobster, but that night, I had a very scary dream. A giant lobster attacked us in our tents. From then on, I stopped eating fish...

I do not have a particular story to tell about the specific moment in time when the conversion to veganism occurred, for it has been a much more gradual process. Concern for the environment, biological diversity, animal welfare, health, sustainable development—these issues have all played a huge role in leading me down this path. And so has the practice of yoga.

Many people see yoga as a form of exercise, another way to keep fit. But yoga is so much more than that. Yoga is a spiritual practice, a state of being. Practicing hatha yoga will keep you fit physically, but that is just a by-product of the practice, not the main goal. The purpose of yoga practice is to unite the body, the mind, the breath, indeed, the self with the universe. The purpose of yoga practice is to know, not intellectually, but experientially, that everything in life is interconnected.

The only guide to how we can achieve this union was given to us by Patanjoli, the father of yoga. According to Patanjoli, yoga has eight limbs. The first two limbs are yama and niyama, which describe an attitude and orientation to one's practice in particular, and to life in general. Yama and niyama each have five elements. The first is ahimsa, typically translated as non-violence. This is the vow that Ghandi took, the vow he lived by.

"Sensitivity" is another way to translate ahimsa, which is how I have been taught by my teacher, Godfrey Devereux. Sensitivity is the core of my practice and how I teach my students. Developing sensitivity is simply a matter of feeling the sensations that arise within you as you practice on your mat, feeling what is actually happening in your body, however small the movement, however subtle the sensation. One has to be able to feel in order to respond appropriately to the sensations arising.

When I first started teaching yoga I felt as though I had abandoned the issues that I care most deeply about—animal welfare and the environment. But I now realize that is not the case. I teach my students to become more sensitive and aware—to really feel what is happening in their bodies on their mats—so they can experience the connection between their physical bodies, their breath and their minds and come to realize that these things are not separate; that we are not separate from each other or from the universe. So, this teaching is yet another way to care for animals and the environment.

At times it has been very painful being so sensitive, as there is so much suffering in this world. But along with the pain, there comes reverence for life—all life. What greater way to demonstrate that reverence than by refusing to use animals for food, clothing or any other purpose. Since purifying my diet from any animal pain or suffering, I seem to have a deep well of compassion for all living creatures, be it a fly or worm or polar bear. I watch with wonder and awe at the spiders spinning their webs, at the snails moving in their shells, at the bees sucking the nectar from flowers, at the beauty of flowers, and all the way up the food chain. I see and feel the inter-connectivity of it all. The miracle of life is so much more awesome when you truly revere all of the individual parts; when you recognize and appreciate the significant role that all beings play in the intricate web of life.

## The Last Fish

*Will Tuttle, Ph.D., composer, pianist, former Zen monk, and author of* The World Peace Diet, *found an undreamed of joy on an adventure that took him as far away as a Zen monastery in Korea.*

I was born into a typical heavy meat and dairy-eating family in New England in the early 1950s, but fortunately discovered the joy of veg-etarianism when I was just 22. Looking back, I can see there were some significant experiences that planted in me the seeds of vegan living. For example, one seed experience from my childhood, that stands out vividly and that I am grateful for having, helped awaken my heart. It was witnessing the killing of a cow on an idyllic Ver-mont dairy farm. I was about twelve years old, and attending a sum-mer camp in the Green Mountains called Camp Challenge.

The camp was affiliated with an organic farm in the valley below us where we would sometimes work baling or weeding. At one point all of us boys went down there. There were horses and cows and fields of beans and wheat under a beautiful blue sky, and we were brought to the barn where a cow was standing alone, in the middle of the wooden floor. She was one of the dairy cows, and Tom (the owner-director of the camp and the farm, a handsome Dartmouth-educated outdoorsman we all admired enormously) informed us that she could not give enough milk and we would therefore be us-ing her for meat. He held a rifle in his hand and pointed to a precise spot on her head where the bullet would have to hit so that she would fall. Then he aimed and fired. I was astounded as the cow instantly crashed to the floor, feces and urine gushing from her rear near where I stood. Tom immediately grabbed a long knife, jumped astride her prostrate body, and with a great strong stroke, cut her head almost completely off. I was amazed at how far the blood shot out of her open neck, propelled by her still-beating heart; long red liquid arcs flying far through the air and splattering all around us as her body convulsed on the blood-soaked floor. We all watched silently as she finally stopped moving and bleeding, and many of us had to wipe our blood-spattered arms and legs. While I stood in shock and horror at what I had just witnessed, Tom wiped his brow and calmly explained that the meat would be no good if her heart didn't pump the blood out of her flesh; it would be soggy and useless. We spent the next hour or so disemboweling her body, and finally got the large edible parts into the back of a truck to be taken to a butcher; we would eat her flesh for the rest of the month. Some of the boys took souvenirs: teats, tail, eyes, brain.

For ten more years, I continued, undaunted, to eat the flesh, milk, and eggs of animals. I simply did not know one could survive without doing so, and I had never met anyone who ate a plant-based diet. When I went away to Colby College in Maine and heard of vegetarianism, something inside me was kindled, but I did not yet question my fundamental eating habits.

In 1974, in my junior year, I heard of The Farm in Tennessee, a relatively newly formed spiritual community of about eight hundred people, mainly from San Francisco. One of the things that intrigued me most about The Farm was that everyone there was a vegetarian. It was a vegan community actually (though that word was not yet in commerce), for they were vegetarian not for health reasons, but for ethical and spiritual reasons, and they ate no animal products whatsoever; not even eggs, dairy products, or honey. I had yet to meet a vegetarian at that point in my life, but I saw in the books published by The Farm pictures of happy, healthy-looking and highly creative people living with a mission to demonstrate a more sustainable and harmonious way of living. I did my senior thesis on Organizational Behavior on The Farm, examining the theory and practice of a community based on cooperation rather than competition, and compassion rather than oppression. It was an eye- and heart-opening project for me. Their purpose was clearly stated: "We're here to help save the world!"

Right after graduating from Colby, my brother Ed and I decided to go on a pilgrimage in search of spiritual understanding. We ended up walking for many months with no money from New England and eventually reached Alabama, going 15 to 20 miles a day on small back-country roads. At one point a friendly man directed us to a quaint little summer cabin on a stream where he said we could spend a few quiet days if we wanted to. We walked there and settled in, but there was no food so we started foraging; and since there were fishing poles there, I decided to catch a few fish.

I put the first fish I caught into my raincoat pocket, and the second into the other, confident they would die before too long. I went back to the cabin to cook supper, quite proud of myself. The cattail roots and wild carrots we had gathered were cooking and I went to clean the fish, but to my dismay they were both still alive and flipping about convulsively. The old patterns kicked in and I grabbed one and slammed him down hard against the floor. Like waking from a nightmare, I could not believe what I was doing. Yet I did not think I could stop. The fish was still alive! Two more times I had to slam him against the floor, and then the other fish as well, before I could clean them, cook them, and we could eat them for dinner.

I could feel their terror and pain, and the violence I was committing against these unfortunate creatures, and I vowed never to fish again. The old programming that they were "just fish" completely fell away, and I saw with fresh eyes what was actually happening. Here I was on a spiritual pilgrimage, trying with all my heart to directly understand the deeper truths of being, yet I was acting contrary to this by first tricking the fish with a lure hiding a cruel barbed hook, and then killing them.

The next day Ed and I walked on, and though I still knew little about being a vegetarian, I began to think it would be a better —even a necessary—way to live. We eventually reached The Farm and stayed there several weeks. The experience absolutely sealed my vegetarianism and was worth the months of walking that it took to get there. Close to a thousand people, mostly living as married couples with kids in self-built homes, had created a community on a large piece of beautifully rolling farm and forest land. It was set up legally as a monastery, and it was strictly vegan to avoid harming animals, people, and the environment. The Farm had its own school, telephone system, soy dairy, publishing company, and Plenty, a blossoming outreach program that provided vegan food and healthcare services both in Central America and in the ghettos of North America. Stephen Gaskin, the spiritual leader, was a student of Zen master Suzuki Roshi, founder of the San Francisco Zen Center.

The food was delicious, the atmosphere unlike anything I had ever experienced. People were friendly, energetic, bright, and there was a powerful sense of purpose: of working to create a better world. The soy dairy made tofu, soy milk, soy burgers, and "Ice Bean", the first soy ice cream, and the schoolhouse for the children served all vegan meals. The kids, vegan from birth, grew tall, strong, and healthy. Gardens, fields, and greenhouses provided food for everyone, and people worked on different crews, building, cooking, teaching, and together making The Farm remarkably self-reliant. I worked in the book printing house.

After several weeks, we decided to continue our journey, walking south eventually to a Korean Zen Center we discovered in Huntsville, Alabama. The Zen training I undertook there led in 1984, nine years later, to my traveling to South Korea with shaved head and robes to live as a Zen monk in an ancient Zen monastery. Though I was a vegetarian, it took this second experience of living in a vegan community to deepen my understanding and commitment to vegan living.

I participated in the summer's three-month intensive retreat. We rose at 2:40 a.m. to begin the day of meditation, practicing silence and simplicity, and eating vegan meals of rice, soup, vegetables, and occasional tofu, and retiring after the evening meditation at

9:00 p.m. The roots of this Korean Zen community in veganism and nonviolence went back about 600 years. There was no silk or leather in any clothing, and it was absolutely not an option to kill even an insect. We simply used a mosquito net in the meditation hall. Through the months of silence and meditation, sitting still for seemingly endless hours, a deep and joyful feeling emerged within, a sense of solidarity with all life and of becoming more sensitive to the energy of situations.

When after four months I returned to the bustle of American life, I felt a profound shift had occurred, and the vegetarianism I'd been practicing for about eight years transformed spontaneously and naturally into veganism with roots that felt as if they extended to the center of my heart. Until then, I had mistakenly thought that my daily vegan purchases of food, clothing, and so forth were my personal choices. Now I could clearly see that not treating animals as commodities was not an option or a choice, for animals simply are not commodities. It would be as unthinkable to eat or wear or justify abusing an animal as it would be to eat or wear or justify abusing a human. The profound relief and empowerment of completely realizing and understanding this in my heart has been enriching beyond words.

*This story is condensed with permission from Lantern Books and Will Tuttle from his book* The World Peace Diet: Eating for Spiritual Health and Social Harmony. *New York: Lantern Books, 2005, pp. 251-264.*

# CHAPTER THREE

## Loving Awakenings

> *Nonviolence is not a garment to be put on*
> *and off at will. Its seat is in the heart, and it must be*
> *an inseparable part of our being.*
> Gandhi

These awakenings never cease to amaze. They come from the smallest event, such as accidentally stepping on a snail, to the largest —visiting a slaughterhouse. One woman personally told me, Tina, of her awakening. She was an omnivore who took her children to McDonald's frequently. One day when her husband returned from hunting, he had a gutted deer strapped to his truck.

She saw the deer lifeless and limp and began to cry, but she could not understand why she was feeling this rush of emotion. She had seen this sort of thing many times before, but the tears came uncontrollably. That night a thought came to her about where the meat in the McDonald's burgers came from and she pictured what she had heard about how cows are slaughtered. She went vegetarian the next day and has not looked back.

Another friend told me of an event that prompted her awakening. She and her children had visited a petting zoo for the afternoon. There were goats, pigs, chickens and other farm animals who were tame and willing to let the little kids hang on them and play with them. That evening when she came home to start dinner and took a package of chicken out, it dawned on her—she had just petted a chicken and the hen was sweet and kind. How could she now eat her? She went vegetarian immediately and threw away the package of chicken.

An especially phenomenal awakening I heard about was from a friend who had a major heart attack. He was 42 years old and nearly died. The doctor treating him told him his arteries were clogged and he needed surgery immediately. This friend had read all of the depressing statistics about the chances of surviving and remaining mentally intact during heart surgery and decided to try it another way. He purchased a copy of *Prevent and Reverse Heart Disease* by Caldwell Esselstyn, Jr., M.D. and six years later, without surgery, is going strong. His arteries are no longer clogged. His cholesterol is 120. To this day he still follows the diet Dr. Esselstyn suggests in his book, and never sways from it. He's proof that a vegan diet can heal.

## Enlightening Dream

*John O'Neill tells of the nightmare that changed his life and the reduction of anger and aggression that he experienced as a result of that change. His story gives us a glimpse of the kind of inner peace that can come to us all from adopting a nonviolent lifestyle and gaining an awareness of the love and beauty of our animal kin.*

Several years ago I began to meet and socialize with a number of vegetarians. They did not engage in judgmental comments, nor give a consistent reason for their dietary practice.

One night the following dream occurred. In the dream I was sitting at my kitchen table in deep despair, for I was cooking my beloved black cat, Crusoe. This cat was the most affectionate, loving animal that ever lived with us. I was going through the litany of the meat eater's rationale: we have to eat, this is how it is done, etc. The cat cried in pain from the pot on the stove. I arose, saying "This is ridiculous! I love this cat and he loves me." I went to retrieve him, but it was too late!

I awoke, profusely sweating, crying, so traumatized that I went immediately to find my feline companion. Finding him, I embraced him in tearful joy. Complete liberation took place; the desire to consume meat was totally gone.

I am not repulsed by the smell nor sight of the cooking of flesh. I am able to enjoy vegan meals with friends eating meat. I feel at peace and harmony within, and it has helped to reduce my anger and aggression.

*O'Neill, John J. Jr. Online Vegetarian Friends journal.*
*"The Peaceable Table", September, 2005, vegetarianfriends.net.*

## Becoming as a Little Child

*Susan Hill Clay tells the story of her step-by-step transformation toward inner peace and spiritual joy. She makes the connection for us between the way little children naturally respond to animals and the spiritual path of "becoming as a little child". Determined to find her spiritual center and a heart at peace, her courageous spiritual journey took her in a surprising direction. She has found peace, not just in helping to liberate animals, but also in helping to educate people about the plight of animals and, thus, help them find their own childlike peace.*

Eight years ago I found myself driving behind a police horse trailer.

Curious, I tailed it to the stables. Its elegant occupant, aptly named Pharoah, emerged, and his officer-and-gentleman rider invited me to visit all 42 horses in the barn. Enamored, I became an instant equine enthusiast.

Seven years ago I learned that my mounted patrol friends, if retired into the wrong hands, could be slaughtered for consumption by horsemeat devotees abroad. Horrified, I became an instant equine rights activist.

Six years ago I discovered that billions of "farmed" animals the world over endure agonizing lives and terrifying deaths. Repulsed, I became an instant vegetarian.

Three years ago I attended a PETA (People for the Ethical Treatment of Animals) conference, where videos showed the sad plight of dairy cows and laying hens, whose milk and eggs I was still consuming. Chastened, I became an instant vegan.

I look back in awe at the moral distance I've traveled in this serendipitous walk alongside my new furred, feathered and finned friends. Changing from comfortable conservative who passively accepted a cultural tradition of eating and wearing animals to passionate crusader bent on bringing them basic legal rights is no small feat in a society fixated on all forms of flesh.

What power transforms an oblivious animal exploiter into an aware animal advocate? In my case, a divinely impelled desire to be made new. Having made morally questionable choices in early adulthood, I longed to return to my spiritual roots—the innocence of my youth. I hankered, in short, to become as a little child.

Many of us recognize that phrase as the advice Christ Jesus gave his disciples when they asked, "Who is the greatest in the kingdom of heaven?" and he replied, "Except ye be converted, and become as little children, ye shall not enter into the kingdom of heaven." (1) Obviously, the Master Christian wasn't suggesting physically shrinking or returning to the helplessness of infancy. He must have meant that attaining peace within—and with all other beings—starts by reclaiming the innocence and integrity embedded in each individual. Achieving harmony, happiness, health, wholeness—the kingdom of heaven on earth—begins, he must have been saying, with rediscovering one's original, unimpeachable childlikeness. Jesus' answer implied that childlikeness and spirituality are identical. That the more childlike one becomes, the more cultivated is one's spirituality.

Becoming as a little child is a lifelong conversion process, not a one-time event. It involves emptying mental closets crammed with selfishness and sensuality. It requires relinquishing entrenched, dead-end habits. It entails sacrificing worldly ambitions, cleansing impure motives. It demands rejecting that pernicious devil variously named conventionality, culture, custom. Becoming as a little child means embracing simplicity and sincerity, meekness and modesty, courage and compassion. It calls for including rather than excluding all living beings. It accepts as normal and natural only the good —whatever blesses all and injures none.

Being introduced to horses...then exposed to members of other species...then educated about the abuses that unenlightened humanity heaps upon these poor creatures—all of these awakenings have sped up my learning curve in spirituality and childlikeness.

But make no mistake. I renounced my former animal-exploiting ways only *after* I had decided to dig up and dust off my child-heart. It was my burning desire for a stronger, more solid spirituality that caused me to follow that trailer to the stables and attracted me to the vibes of pure love felt in that barn full of horses. From that pivotal day on, my growing spiritual sense steered me into making ever more animal-friendly decisions. For example, this spiritual sense caused me to recognize the utter hypocrisy of protecting some animals while killing others—a sort of self-deceit inconceivable to the child-heart. It's no wonder I now relate to this statement made by spiritual pioneer Mary Baker Eddy: "Willingness to become as a little child and to leave the old for the new, renders thought receptive of the advanced idea. Gladness to leave the false landmarks and joy to see them disappear—this disposition helps to precipitate the ultimate harmony. The purification of sense and self is a proof of progress. 'Blessed are the pure in heart: for they shall see God.'" (2)

My receptivity to the "advanced idea" of how humans should

treat animals has been enhanced through countless hours of reading, thinking, and listening for answers from Above. An "advanced idea", I've concluded, has to be progressive and metaphysical. It can't be bound by either tradition or by the physical senses and their interpretation of reality. So, to advance spiritually, I had to get beyond seeing animals traditionally—as physical beings, as dispensable commodities, as inferior to and the property of humans.

One of my revelations was that the true substance, and therefore usefulness, of animals consists entirely of their good qualities—their native intelligence, endless forgiveness, rich creativity, uncontaminated honesty. Seeing that, I could no longer regard them as useful for the flesh and fur they are forced to give up to feed and clothe a supposedly superior species.

I say "supposedly superior" because part of my eye-opening growth involved seeing through that myth. As a pupil in a Christian Science Sunday School, I'd been assured that man having dominion means being good stewards for God's animals and earth. But I never grasped how man could be the "greater" and animals the "lesser" outcome of God. After all, how could the Originator of us all be capable of originating any species *inferior* to the Original! And how could a loving Parent bestow less affection on some of His-Her offspring than on others?

A few months ago it finally hit me: animals must be "lesser" *only* in one way. They possess less of one facet of God— "less of Mind" (3). To me, Mind, when capitalized, describes our Creator. And, specifically, Mind describes His capacity to know all there is to know about the perfection of His "very good" creation (Genesis 31:1). Suddenly, it made sense to me. Man is created as the ultimate and exact expression of creative Mind, mirroring Mind's comprehension of All —Mind's comprehensiveness. However, in no other aspect of God's nature are animals "lesser". In many respects they are often perhaps "greater" expressions of other aspects of God maybe partly because they are unencumbered by the challenges of the Mind component.

For instance, it's obvious to any spiritually attuned observer that animals manifest the *complete* range of what some might call God's "Soul" characteristics—that is, Soul's grace, harmony, beauty, purity, innocence. Similarly, they portray the *full* complement of our Maker's "Truth" traits, such as authenticity, loyalty, and trustworthiness. Equally, every living being I can think of possesses the *entire* measure of God's "Life" attributes, from ongoing activity and perpetual motion to continual newness and development. As for the "Spirit" side of our Source, expressed as animation, energy, exuberance...well, how many creatures do you know that aren't *full* of it! Spirit, that is. And creatures big and small certainly embrace every single one of God's "Love" virtues, from mothering care to altruistic generosity.

Another breakthrough I've had is the realization that animals' spiritual and moral identity is not susceptible to materiality and evil. I see this identity as both harmless and incapable of being harmed or destroyed. From my vantage point, the trenchant truth, "Nothing that lives ever dies, and *vice versa*," (4) is as applicable to the animals as to man. Meaning that we're all immortal! This knowledge comforts me when I'm faced with the sad mortal scene of creatures, considered our "property", our "possessions", suffering under the hand of tyrannical, irresponsible or ignorant "owners".

Becoming vegan is simply one effect of my increased spirituality. I don't focus on my new consumption choices. In fact, I purposely put very little time, thought or money into meals or clothes. This philosophy is in keeping with both my Spartan early-retirement lifestyle and my release, some 20 years ago, from a long-standing addiction to food.

The mere act of eating a plant-based diet doesn't improve the spiritual muscle of the eater, nor does it enlighten the world. To effect meaningful, lasting change, the decision to become vegan must be rooted in the ethic of respect for all beings. Earth is uplifted only by pure motives and good thoughts, manifested in kind deeds done for others. Acts performed for self-centered, fear-based or materially minded reasons (an obsession with nutrition, calories, body shape, disease prevention) are without real love, thus neither redemptive nor permanent.

The outward reformation (my implementing the "advanced idea") that has flowed from my inner transformation (my "willingness to become as a little child") has at times felt wrenching, uncomfortable, solitary. Stepping out of a culture steeped in 10,000 years of carnivorism has meant that I no longer see eye to eye with many friends and family members. There have been a few tense moments, a few exchanges of unfortunate words. But the same divinely prompted love that inspired my longing to be made new spiritually, to be converted to childlikeness, has gradually harmonized my interactions with others. As a result of desiring to be fed daily by divine Love, I can honestly say that I no longer despise those who knowingly hurt and kill animals. And I've largely stopped being angry and impatient with the ignorant, unwitting accomplices of that abuse. Instead, I feel compassion for them all, recognizing that the latter are where I was a short time ago.

Perhaps because I have been so willing, even eager, to let Spirit guide me and show me how to right my wrongs toward Her creatures, my reformed heart has evolved into a reformer's heart. I continually ask Love to lead me to Her receptive child-hearts who are ready to be made new. I ask Truth to help me awaken those who want to open their eyes to the light of love for all beings.

My newfound mission as a reformer demands that I keep growing in order to keep going. When I'm tempted to falter or believe I'm not cut out for the work, I'm given exactly what I need to boost my confidence and enthusiasm.

One of the precious gifts I've received takes the form of a few simple words buried in a magazine article. The author lists five bullet points for tracking spiritual growth. Every time I read two of these reminders, they lighten my load and cheer me onward and upward:

1. "Become a reformer. Reformers are not usually popular, and it takes energy to forward constructive change. We can all feel tremendous pressure to leave the human scene unstirred. But unwillingness to forward reform is really a form of selfishness, and if we cave to that unwillingness, everyone's progress stops sooner or later, including our own. Spiritual growth means we continuously examine what we believe and how we behave. And thereby we become more energized by being more Christlike."

2. "Move beyond the desire to labor only for the benefit of ourselves and those closest to us. As we grow in our love for others, we can embrace reform as a constant. We will discover ways to bring healing that we never thought possible. We may discover unused talents or find that the respect we've gained encourages people to listen to what we say and to grow themselves." (5)

Yes, to grow into little children. As I am becoming, and being.

## Love for a Little Bird

*Madeleine Tuttle travels with her husband, Will Tuttle, full time in an RV (recreational vehicle), giving workshops and painting visionary art. Together they are spreading the message of love and peace to all beings. In her story she explains how a childhood trauma led to a life-changing decision.*

On a sunny day when I was about five years young, I walked from where I lived near Lake Geneva in Switzerland past my favorite shop, a bicycle rental where my mother would sometimes gift me with an afternoon of delightful bicycling. But on this particular day, a painful experience waited around the corner. What I saw was a small dead bird, and since he had gotten hit by something, his body had broken open and showed his inner organs.

I was deeply shocked. Tears started running down my cheeks as I looked down upon this poor bird. With a heart full of grief, I ran back home to my mother and shared with her my aching heart. At the same time, she had lunch ready...oh-oh! Spaghetti and tomato sauce with meat bits...

This sight made me cry even more. And I exclaimed to her that I couldn't eat this, since this looked like the dead bird I had just seen. I declared that I wouldn't eat anything ever that looked like that bird.

My mother was not alarmed by my demand. Because she accepted my decision, I was spared having animals on my plate as I grew up. My two older brothers, though, seemed happy to eat the meat she regularly served. I later learned that my grandmother also shared my mother's respect for vegetarianism. I think many children wouldn't eat animals if they weren't forced by their elders to do so.

There were a couple of years in my life when I prepared meat dishes. If I didn't "salt and spice" them in the beginning stages of cooking them, I nearly threw up standing in the kitchen. Eating meat is another question. If the flesh was more camouflaged, it was easier to eat, since it didn't remind me of my little dead bird friend I had encountered when I was five.

My early childhood vegetarian experience wasn't lost though. In my late twenties, thirty years ago, I made the decision to never eat animals again. In fact I went further and became a vegan, and I'm so happy I did. Every meal is a celebration!

The little bird in the story left me with a tender heart, and this tender heart has taught me a lot along the way. Life is sacred, and since I can't create it, there is no question in my mind that I should not destroy it. This knowledge embraces me with a sense of peace.

Preparing food has become a more and more joyous activity for me. It's creative and very much a spiritual act. It is painting, modeling, and working with Spirit's infinite arising of forms, colors and energy. In other words, preparing food is a meditation, but how could it be so if I were cooking the bodies of innocent animals.

Thanks to my mother for her understanding! She also became a vegan about ten years ago, and now in her eighties says she feels healthier than ever.

I am an artist. Drawing and painting, which have accompanied me throughout life, make up some of the main ways in which I express and share my love for the world and work toward its healing. For the last fifteen years especially, animals have called to me and received first priority as subjects in my art.

I definitely feel that being vegan helps me on my spiritual path. It's more straightforward. I don't have to select which animals I would kill and which ones I would caress. It's ethical, but also aesthetical, which is very important to me, as an artist.

*For further biographical information and examples of Madeleine Tuttle's art, see willtuttle.com.*

## Dog on the Menu

*Marine Lieutenant-Colonel Robert Lucius looked into the eyes of a dog and was changed forever.*

I had been serving as the Marine Corps attaché to the U.S. Embassy in Hanoi, Vietnam, when I received the task of delivering a shipment of medical supplies to Lai Chau Province. On the way, I saw something that will haunt me forever. We passed a lone motorbike, and strapped to the back was a wicker cage with four full-grown dogs stuffed inside. The cage might have been comfortable for one. One of the dogs looked right at me, and I felt his fear and dread. I wanted to buy the dogs and set them free, but as I hemmed and hawed, they were long gone.

Later that day, I was treated to lunch at a small café as a token of appreciation for the medical donation. As I was leaving, I walked past the kitchen. Splayed out on the floor was a dead, skinned dog. In my mind I saw the dog's eyes again. I have seen a lot of things in my 18 years of military service, but I never felt like a coward until that moment. My hesitation cost four lives. On that day, I became a vegetarian, and when I told my wife my story, she eventually did too.

*Lucius, Robert. "Suddenly it hit me…", PETA's (People for the Ethical Treatment of Animals) Summer, 2007, issue of* Animal Times *magazine.*

Lieutenant-Colonel Lucius was kind enough to give us an update recently. As you can see, he and his wife have continued to be inspired to help animals. He explained, "It has been a while since that story was published, and life has continued to surprise me. My wife and I both have remained vegetarian and are transitioning toward vegan. I volunteer now at the local ASPCA and when I retire in two years I will devote my full-time efforts to the establishment of animal sanctuaries and humane education programs in Vietnam and Indonesia! I would not have guessed that three years ago, but it just goes to show how a single moment can change a life."

# CHAPTER FOUR

# Animals and Energy Fields

*The mind is incapable of vibrating at the higher frequencies and
manifesting the higher aspects of mind, when a person eats dead flesh.*
Charles Fillmore, cofounder of Unity Church

We are learning through both science and spirituality that we are all
interconnected. As John Muir once said, "When we try to pick out
anything by itself, we find that it is bound fast, by a thousand invisible cords that cannot be broken, to everything in the universe."

War against people anywhere on the globe, for example, impacts
the energy field and spiritual life of every living being on the planet.
Likewise, the ongoing war against animals has a violating and destructive effect on each one of us.

*Vegan Inspiration's* author and chef Todd Dacey suggests that,

"To choose cruelty-free, light, health-promoting, simple meals, prepared with love and caring, is an important part of the solution. These healthy food choices are often the first step to a greater ability to tune into life's great mystery and to experience the profound revealing of who we are as individual cells interconnected within the universal body of creation."

Will Tuttle points out that the incredible magnitude of the human-caused destruction on the planet is a result of "our inner desensitization to vibrational energy frequencies—the numbness that keeps us from screaming or weeping when we bite into a hot dog or cheeseburger".

Eating food from animals causes restlessness, anger, and anxiety, according to Gabriel Cousens, while a plant-based diet quiets the mind and opens the heart to universal love. Meat, dairy products, eggs, fast foods, microwaved meals, and alcohol have no life force in them. He believes that the energy fields of these foods are so disrupted that they significantly decrease and damage the life force and the consciousness of those who eat them. Any food from animals is filled with the fear, brutality, and disrespect that accompanied their lives and deaths.

This is consistent with what Theosophist Charles Leadbeater saw in the energy fields of those who consumed animal flesh. According to him, there was a dense cloudiness around the physical bodies of meat eaters compared to people whom he observed eating only non-animal foods. Likewise, Annie Besant, another famous Theosophist, wrote passionately about her train ride into Chicago in the early 1900s. She described an oppressive sense of desolation that she attributed to the dark energy of terror and pain emanating from the Chicago stockyards. (1)

Marjorie Emerson adopted an ahimsa lifestyle and became vegan in order "to raise my vibrations to be a better healer. Each higher level of training required a 'higher' level of food intake—strict vegetarian diet for those at the highest level". (2)

The stories in this chapter were shared with us by people who experienced this energy connection in various and profound ways.

It is through their generosity in communicating their stories that we may come to a deeper understanding that everything we do affects everyone and everything. Therefore, let us cultivate compassion, kind hearts, and ahimsa in every possible way.

As Gabriel Cousens so aptly said, "We eat to enhance our Communion with the Divine," and that leads us to an inner peace that will no longer be missing, but will be instead an intrinsic and permanent part of our lives.

## The Shaman and the Very Sad Cow

*Eckhart Tolle, author of* The New Earth *and* The Power of Now, *recommends that when we sit down to a meal, we tune in to what is on our plates and feel the vibration of each type of food. Does it feel light and loving, or does it feel dark, damaged, and full of pain? While we are eating the food, we can continue to sense how we are reacting to it emotionally.*

*Doreen Virtue, author of* Eating in the Light: Making the Switch to Vegetarianism on Your Spiritual Path, *even suggests that when we go to the grocery store, we can pass our hands over the items we intend to buy and ask ourselves, or even the food itself, if it will nurture us. If our hands feel cold or we feel a negative gut reaction, it is an indication that it is a food that will bring us the same pain or disharmony that is in the food itself.*

One day I, Judy, was visiting with a shaman who lives not far from my home. We were discussing energy fields—a subject very familiar to shamans. As we talked, it occurred to me to ask him what sort of energy fields he sensed in and around his food. He told me a story that brought me to tears. He had always been a meat eater, but as his awareness of energy fields and the interconnection of all life was growing, he decided one day to tune in to his meal which contained cow meat. Being careful about where his food came from, he knew that this particular cow had been raised with greater care and attention than most cows. Still, he decided to feel the vibration coming

63

from the meat on his plate. As soon as he did so, he experienced the cow's anguish and pain from the time she was forcefully taken from her mother.

The shaman also experienced the terror she felt when she was being brutally killed. This man went ahead and ate the meat, but it was the last time for him. That night he became very ill and understood that he could no longer take the suffering of others into his own body.

## Angels' Peace

*Doreen Virtue, workshop leader and author of many books, prayed for guidance and received a puzzling message that led her to a life of ahimsa and greater clairvoyance and intuition.*

When I began devoting my private practice to conducting spiritual counseling, I asked for Divine guidance on how to increase my clairvoyance. I immediately saw, in my mind's eye, an image of chicken meat pieces. I figured that my guides misunderstood my question, so I asked again, "What steps can I take to increase the vividness of my clairvoyance?" Again, I saw a mental picture of raw chicken meat.

This made no sense to me, so I asked my guides to clarify what they meant by this image. Immediately, I heard them say, "You are blocking your clairvoyance by eating chicken, since you are absorbing the energy of pain when you eat it." This seemed bizarre, almost unbelievable to me, so I asked a more experienced clairvoyant for confirmation of my Divine guidance. He validated that many people who are interested in developing their psychic abilities are guided to drop meat from their diets.

Since that time, I have adopted a vegan diet, which means that I don't eat any animal products. My clairvoyance has dramatically improved, and I feel wonderful.

At my workshops, I help audience members hear the voice of their angels. One of the questions that they ask their angels is "How can I improve my ability to see and hear you?" About half the time, the angels say, "You're eating too much cheese (or milk, or some other dairy product)." The angels explain that dairy products clog the psychic senses. Excessive dairy shows up in the aura, looking like a milky cloud surrounding the person, with a greasy feel to it.

Since animal products contain a low life-force energy, they slow the chakras. Increased psychic and intuitive abilities are one of the many benefits of adopting a vegetarian diet.

*Virtue, Doreen, and Perlitz, Becky.* Eating in the Light: Making the Switch to Vegetarianism on Your Spiritual Path. *Carlsbad, CA: Hay House, 2001, pp. 43–45.*

## The Kinship of Kittens

*Lisa Kay Adam, a vegetarian from Texas, tells us how the animals she knows and loves help her join with them in an egoless state of presence and pure awareness. Perhaps they are little mystics and yogis in disguise.*

While still in high school, I overheard the mother of another student complain, "All he does is play with his kitty cat!" Not only was I surprised that this he-man football player had a kitten, I was surprised that anyone found this activity so objectionable.

The older I become, the more I find play with my cats and other animals to be a spiritual exercise. Play, more than petting or training animals, engages and refreshes me. While stroking their fur, I may daydream or ruminate. If I am training or grooming an animal, my mind is at work on an objective. But when a cat and I tensely lock eyes over a twitching string, I experience a wonderful suspension of ego. Our play provides me with a pause in the stream of consciousness that I recognize as "self". That pause—"the pause that refreshes", to borrow an advertisement line—allows me to dip into a state rare in hectic life.

In a favorite novel, *Immortality*, a soul-weary character decides that what is painful isn't "being, but being one's self". The self is a burden, she thinks, but being is a refreshing fountain. Lying unaware beside a murmuring stream, she joins with "primordial being".

To me, that primordial being is God. From my faith tradition, it is the "living waters" and the "fountain of life", but people of many faiths share this conception.

Lal Ded, a Kashmiri mystic, wrote of "the lake [from which] all Beings drink". "Into it deer, jackals, rhinoceri, sea-elephants falling," she extolled, "from the earliest moment of birth, falling and falling in You". Like Lal Ded, I share a sense of kinship with the world's many beings, all dependent upon living waters. Daily life muddies and obscures this joyful kinship; moments of play with animals reveal it in instant clarity.

Of course, absorbed play with a kitten is not the only way to experience this state, and I know that, for some people, it is not something religious. For many, it may be like the "flow" that psychologist Mihály Csíkszentmihályi described, a mental state of satisfying and self-forgetting immersion in activity. Meditation, prayer, painting, even driving, allow different people to escape occasionally their wearying awareness of self. Playing with animals, like gardening, has the additional advantage of engaging us with living creation.

It is miraculous to me that humans can connect with other species, beings with their own inviolable, precious, and fundamentally mysterious essences. Despite innumerable days alongside my pet companions, I know that in them are whole worlds of sensation, thought, and, yes, feeling, beyond my comprehension.

Self-forgetting, connection, and mystery are parts of religion that animals allow me to experience. Such concepts, however, are part of my conscious vocabulary. While romping joyfully with a dog, weighty thoughts are replaced with light-hearted unawareness. After our play, I feel refreshed, as if we had bathed in a bubbly, deep, and infinitely rejuvenating spring of water.

*Adam, Lisa Kay, from "The Francis Files"*
*of The Humane Society of the United States, hsus/religion.org.*

## To Be More Psychic

*Erin Pavlina (erinpavlina.com) is known for her psychic abilities now, but there was a time when burgers and fries were getting in her way.*

I grew up on fast food dinners. My mom really hated cooking and saw no problem with feeding me and my siblings junk food. I didn't care; I was the envy of all my friends who had to eat home-cooked meals and ugh, vegetables! I was sickly growing up though, and by the time I was eighteen my cholesterol levels were through the roof.

In college something began to change. As I became more aware of what was going on in the world I decided that I really wanted to make a difference in bringing our planet back to a state of love, peace, harmony, and compassion. I remember asking my spirit guides what I had to do to achieve this goal. They responded with, "Stop eating animal flesh." What? What does that have to do with anything, I wondered. But they insisted that this was the answer. I told them, "No way. I don't want to, nor do I think I could give up beef, chicken or fish." They quieted down.

As time went on I continued to check in with my guides and higher self and asked them to help me become powerful in some way so I could help the planet. Again and again they told me I had to stop eating animals. I finally asked them why, and they told me that it lowered my vibration to ingest matter that was in a state of fear and agony when it died. They told me the food carried the emotional residue of that pain and suffering, and that eating it would lower my vibration. They explained that if I wanted the ability to help people and our planet, I needed to stop eating animal flesh. I remember telling them that this might be so, but I could not do it. They were very patient and kind.

In my mid-20s I met my future husband, Steve Pavlina, who was already a vegetarian. He never seemed deprived when eating and I began to wonder if it was possible I could enjoy being vegetarian. I decided to try it, and when I did, I loved it! I felt noticeably better. Before we got married, Steve told me he wanted to try going vegan

—no animal products in the diet whatsoever. I told him that was too hard and certainly a cruel way to raise children. But I decided I had to try it for thirty days just to be sure. After seven days I was hooked. I absolutely loved being vegan. I could think more clearly, my skin cleared up, chronic conditions I'd had for years went away, my anxiety went away, and I lost lots of weight. After thirty days I was a new person in body, mind, and spirit. And it was a lot easier than I ever imagined it would be.

Shortly after going vegan I noticed my psychic abilities were increasing. I could more clearly hear my spirit guides. I would get premonitions more frequently and more accurately. I was better able to sense what people were thinking and feeling. In time, I was able to raise my vibration high enough to communicate with the deceased.

I know that eliminating animal products from my diet played a huge role in increasing my psychic abilities. I don't believe you absolutely have to go vegan in order to become a good psychic, but it worked for me. To live your life compassionately and in congruence with the highest good of all creatures raises your vibration, and when your vibration is high enough you begin to be able to sense and communicate with higher vibrational beings.

My spirit guides were pleased that I finally got their message, and I was rewarded with a great gift. Today I am able to reach hundreds of thousands of people with my blog, and I am an intuitive counselor, helping people find their true purpose in life and move away from problems that plague them. For me, going vegan was the first step in my journey to help heal our planet. I am grateful I finally listened to the wisdom of my spirit guides.

# CHAPTER FIVE

## How Animals Help Us Awaken

*Could you look an animal in the eyes and say to [him or her]:*
*"My appetite is more important than your suffering?"*
Moby

I, Judy, was sailing with my husband on a trimaran off the eastern coast of the Baja peninsula. We were sailing at night in order to arrive at our destination at dawn when we could better make out the landmarks we needed for safe harbor.

It was exhilarating beyond anything I'd ever experienced. At first, things seemed to be going along well, but then the wind came up and waves started crashing over the bow. I could feel myself beginning to panic, but I knew I had to remain calm. I said a prayer, and the waves got bigger. However, within seconds of my prayer, a flash of white caught my eye.

I looked, and there in the glow of our stern light, a brilliant white gull flew—staying perfectly even with our boat and also staying in the light where I could see her. How can one explain a "knowing"? It is just something you feel so deeply that no one can talk you out of it. I "knew" that gull had come to help me. How did she know I needed her, and how did she arrive so quickly? She stayed near to me for as long as it took for me to become completely calm and full of peace. I "knew" that she had come to calm me and care for me. Somehow, she communicated to me—"Look at me. I am safe here on this windy sea, and because I am safe, you are safe. We are in God's loving arms now and always. Have no fear. Love is everywhere present."

No one knows how many people have been saved from drowning, and shark attacks, by dolphins, yet human beings kill millions of dolphins each year and enslave many others in the "entertainment" industry. Whales, also the target of human greed for centuries, have saved many an unfortunate sailor. Just about everyone knows a story of a dog who has rescued a person, but few know that pigs, horses, cows, monkeys, birds, and many other animals have done the same.

But beyond the saving of our physical lives, perhaps the most entrancing, mysterious, and thought-provoking sort of help we get from animals is spiritual and emotional. Though the reason for this help may elude us at this point in our development, we cannot help but wonder if animals are divine messengers, far more in tune with God than we, and willing, whenever called upon, to touch a needy, hurting heart and heal it. Cody—part chow, part golden retriever— comes to visit us almost every day from his farm house down the road. When I look into his eyes, I see God, for God is unconditional love, and that love just beams and shines from Cody's eyes.

The lesson learned from animals is clear. If we harm or kill them, we suffer great spiritual grief, unconscious though it may be. When we see them as our planetary relations, worthy of our respect and love, the love and peace that envelops us is beyond measure.

## Then I Met "Chicken"

*It took a little chicken showing love to awaken Jennifer Rotondo to the realization that chickens not only have personalities but can sometimes even be heroes.*

Jennifer Rotondo, an editor for *The Observer Dispatch*, was so moved by the heroic action of a little chicken that she felt the need to write an article in her publication about it.

Early in her life she had loved cows and pigs so much that she did not eat them. However, as she explained it, she was still "able to separate poultry from the other animals". But that was to change when she reached the age of sixteen.

At that time her boyfriend Tom purchased a chick to feed to his pet python. The chick was so adorable that it was difficult for Tom to put her into the python's cage. Nevertheless, he did, but to his and Jennifer's amazement the chick was too quick for the snake. Tom was so impressed with this little "scrapper" that he took her out of the cage, and she became a part of the family. He named her Chicken.

"She developed a distinct personality," wrote Rotondo, "and preferred certain people to others. She would meet you at the car when you pulled into the driveway." However, the event that ended chicken-eating forever for this teenager was yet to come.

One day Jennifer and Tom were walking in his unfenced yard with his niece, who was just a toddler. A large dog started coming toward them growling and appearing quite threatening. The two teens picked up the baby and began to walk quickly toward the house. At this point the menacing dog began to run toward them.

It was then that Chicken showed her heroic nature. "Chicken swooped in, flying erratically, hopping and flapping her wings while pecking at the dog's face." This confused and distracted the dog so much that he ran away. And Chicken resumed her normal day, pecking in the grass, as if she had done nothing extraordinary.

Through this, Jennifer saw first hand that "chickens are smart, social creatures that form bonds with each other and protect their families. And I," wrote Jennifer, "am living proof."

*Rotondo, Jennifer. "Observer-Dispatch", posted online May 22, 2008. Rotondo is Weekend Plus editor for the Observer.*

## The Story of Queenie

She made a daring dash from a New York City slaughterhouse in Queens and won the hearts of thousands of people who joined her quest for freedom.

We're talking, of course, about Queenie, a young cow who was slated for slaughter at Astoria Live Poultry, a meat market that keeps live animals and allows customers to choose the animals they want butchered. After hearing the screams of other animals, Queenie made her own choice—a choice any animal would make in the same situation if given a chance. After escaping from the slaughterhouse, she ran several blocks through the streets of New York City, surprising motorists and passers-by. Though she avoided capture at first, the five-hundred-pound cow was finally caught after a wild chase with NYPD cars, local authorities, and a tranquilizer gun.

Gene Bauston (now Baur), Director of Farm Sanctuary, reported on her heroic escape to freedom: "Queenie's freedom dash was quickly picked up by the media—and her story spread throughout the country. Queenie's courageous escape was featured on national television, and millions of viewers saw a frightened cow running from the slaughterhouse, clearly aware of the fate that had awaited her. Hundreds of calls poured into The Center for Animal Care and Control and Astoria Live Poultry, urging both the agency and the slaughterhouse owner to release the animal to a sanctuary where she could live out the remainder of her life.

"Alerted to the cow's plight by Farm Sanctuary members, we immediately contacted the animal control agency and offered to provide Queenie a safe, loving, permanent home. For several hours, it was unclear if the agency would obtain custody of the cow, but public sentiment and pressure paid off—and the slaughterhouse owner agreed to give the cow to the city. In statements to newspapers, Aladdin El-sayed, owner of Astoria Live Poultry, which is a halal slaughterhouse stated, 'God was willing to give it a new life, so why wouldn't I?' (*Newsday*). El-sayed also stated he had paid $500 for the cow, and had been fined $1,000 for causing an 'animal nuisance'. The Health Department may fine him an additional $2,000. El-sayed claimed he 'lost a lot of money', but that it didn't matter because, in his own words, 'There is something with this cow.' (*Daily News*)

"After receiving the word on Friday afternoon that Queenie would be given to Farm Sanctuary, our animal transport vehicle was rolling to New York City by Friday night. We picked up Queenie from the JFK Airport where she was being held, and drove her directly to our New York shelter. Queenie jumped off the trailer amid cheers from the sanctuary staff…and loud 'welcome' moo's from the shelter cows.

"Queenie has put a face on vegetarianism. With news stories on the major television networks, Associated Press, and articles in *The New York Times*, *New York Daily News*, and dozens of other newspapers, millions of people have learned that farm animals have feelings too.

"Queenie's quest has also launched a neighborhood effort to close the slaughterhouse. Like Queenie seizing her moment for freedom, residents have seized the news media to draw attention to their demand to close the meat market. Among their concerns reported in the *New York Post*, residents stated, 'This is a market that we don't believe is treating anything humanely, and we want to see it closed for that reason alone…Through the night, you can hear the screaming of the animals. I don't know what they are doing to them.'"

Queenie knew, and now the rest of the world knows, too.

*Volpe, Tina, reprinted from* The Fast Food Craze: Wreaking Havoc on Our Bodies and Our Animals, *Canyon Publishing, LLC.*

## Smitten by a Kitten

*Eddie Lama, a tough-minded, New York City construction contractor was trying to get a date with a woman who just happened to be looking for a pet-sitter. Although Eddie disliked animals, he thought it would impress her if he took care of her cat while she was away. Little did he know that in the next few days, his entire life would be turned upside down. This one little kitten began to open his heart.*

*Eddie started watching the kitten with fascination. He was so playful and affectionate. Within a few days, this little cat awakened him to a whole new world of animals and animal consciousness. His entire perception of animals shifted.*

*Eddie began rescuing animals off the streets of New York and finding them homes. As he grew to know and love each one of them, he had another awakening. While petting one of the cats he noticed how much her leg felt like a chicken's leg. That evening he went to his brother's house for dinner, and they were serving chicken. He couldn't eat the chicken, because he had made that mind-blowing connection between the pets whom we don't eat and the animals whom we do eat. They are all the same in their desire to live and be loved.*

*Naturally he became a vegan. He also quit a 20-year smoking habit when he noticed that the smoke caused one of the cats to cough. The next step in his journey of expanding compassion was to begin participating in animal advocacy rallies, marches, and outreach events. Eventually, as a result of his passion to help animals and his inventive nature, he put together the FaunaVision van. This van traveled the streets of New York city showing videos of the plights of animals on TV screens mounted on the van. Activists everywhere, inspired by Eddie, developed smaller mobile units and other vans to bring the truth of what is happening to animals to the people. Eddie also founded the Oasis Sanctuary.*

*The award-winning documentary, The Witness (tribeofheart.org), chronicles Eddie's journey from a violent world to a life of compassion and animal advocacy. This unique documentary has been called "the most persuasive and important documentary film ever made".*

*The following speech was given by Eddie at a Witness screening in London:*

...I know that many of you lead busy lives and may think that there are more important things to do than to sit here and watch a movie about furry critters. After all there is a war going on, so do we really need to worry about pigs and foxes and cows and cats? What about the children, the refugees, the starving and the dispossessed —shouldn't they be the focus of our efforts? Does it really make a difference if we stop hurting animals? Can we end human suffering by giving a damn about critters? The answer is yes.

What you saw here tonight is not necessarily a movie about animals as much as it is about the principles and concepts of compassion and nonviolence. Compassion is defined as sympathetic consciousness of others' distress together with a desire to alleviate it.

After all what is compassion if it is applied selectively? It's a form of an 'ism, no? Can we claim to love children if we only love white children? Can we claim to be peace lovers, but only as it applies to our own country?

There is also the idea of bearing witness to wrong-doing and speaking out against it. Currently in NYC there is an advertising campaign that urges the public to inform the appropriate authorities if they suspect something potentially harmful is going on. The tag line is: "If you see something say something." It is a media push by my government to help local authorities prevent terrorist attacks. I have not been in your wonderful city for about three years but I understand there is a similar message being presented to the people here. I think it is an imperative duty of all human beings to say something if they see something is wrong. It is this idea that has compelled me to action, in many ways by personal experience. Back in the seventies I was a victim of wrong-doing. Three people tried to kill me during a robbery related incident. (It was not all disco you know!) No one heard my pleas and no one came to my rescue and no one came forward. The crime went unpunished and the perpetrators went about wreaking their violence upon others seemingly with impunity. Since then I have often thought that if someone had said something, their reign of terror would have at least been shortened and maybe fewer people would have been hurt.

The ugliness of evil can only exist in the dark. Bearing witness and saying something shines a light on it. Being a voice brings with it a message that something is unacceptable. Gradually a particular ugly act becomes a source of shame and in turn makes it less salable to people of goodwill. It is much like slave ownership. It was once a measure of success but is now seen as a gauge of brutality and insensitivity.

There is a saying that goes, and I will paraphrase, that *truth* undergoes three phases before it is accepted as such. First it is ridiculed; then it is violently opposed; and finally it becomes self-evident. In my experience I have found this to be true. I think with the concept of animal rights we are at the second stage, with barely a toe into the third phase. We may not be able to end the atrocities in Darfur; or be rid of the oppressive nature of the Taliban; or end the war in Iraq; or the brutal occupation of the Palestinian people. No single action can do that. However, we can end the horrors and violence in our own lives by being mindful of the unheard suffering of our fellow-beings with just one act, right now, and that is by going vegan.

We can help alleviate the suffering of many sentient beings right away. This is something that is not as easily accomplished in the area of human suffering. So for me the areas of human rights and animal rights are not mutually exclusive but rather, inextricably intertwined within the concepts of compassion and nonviolence. It is not necessary to first end all human maladies before we address animal issues. In fact, a veggie diet will very likely extend one's life allowing the opportunity for one to advocate longer on human issues, how about that? Well, you have the idea.

Again I want to thank everyone for caring enough to be here. I will end this already too long soliloquy by quoting my best friend and Oasis sanctuary co-founder, the great, late Eddie Rizzo's favorite line: "The job of a good citizen is to keep one's mouth open."

P.S. In case you're wondering—all went well with the woman who introduced me to the cat, but the real love story lies with the animals. It's amazing what being smitten by a kitten can do—maybe change your life.

## Lauren's Lesson

*Kay Pfaltz (kaypfaltz.com) is the author of a lovely book entitled* Lauren's Story: An American Dog in Paris. *In her book one finds, possibly, the best description of that special bond between a dog and the person she or he loves. Those who read Kay's book and have not experienced the unconditional love and deep connection that animals can offer us will find it so beautifully explored and explained, they may well find themselves on their way to the local animal shelter to rescue one. Those who have experienced that dear and unforgettable connection will be forever grateful to Kay for putting it into words and indeed validating it. This mysterious and wonderful love that crosses the species barrier is absolutely real and, for some, the greatest gift on earth. As an example, here is a wonderful passage from Kay's book:*

"I looked over at Lauren there beside me like always. Her face was now all white. She looked up and into my eyes. In all my life, I have never known such sustained happiness as that which I've felt when with her. I realized my gratitude had not only to encompass past and future, but present, and in this moment was perfection."

*While Kay's book chronicles her travels with Lauren, her beloved beagle, it also touches upon her work as a restaurant critic and the many cafés where she and Lauren dined in Paris. But something amazing happened to this woman who once called herself a "raving carnivore". Lauren's unconditional love for Kay began opening up a space in her heart for other animals. In her "Afterword" to the third printing of* Lauren's Story, *Kay explains what happened next.*

When I wrote *Lauren's Story* I was still a gourmand and raving carnivore. One of my greatest pleasures was sitting down in a bistro and ordering an elaborate—usually several courses—yet simple meal. I knew how to order like the French. And I knew how to eat. This pleased both me and many a waiter...

[However, over time, I came to understand] if we dog-lovers look in our dog's eyes and know he or she has a soul it seems obvious then that all animals do and that all animals are capable of feeling love, affection, pain or fear, no different from our dogs and cats. Yet the vast majority of farm animals lead abominable lives and we can no longer pretend this isn't so just because it's convenient to (our desires and pleasures beg us to turn a blind eye), or inconvenient not to (whatever would we serve for dinner?). There is something wrong when dogs are flying on planes to Paris, dining out in restaurants or sleeping on plush pillows and ten billion farm animals never know one good day of life. Often we, the consuming public, perpetrate crimes against animals through ignorance. By educating ourselves to what is really happening behind the closed doors of the factory farm, I believe we can change this and move towards sustainable farming.

For these and other reasons I am now a vegetarian—something that seems antithetical to the French mentality of eating and dining and food itself, for not only are the French a nation of meat eaters, but the connotations surrounding the term "vegetarian" are the very things that make the French cringe and think badly of Americans: diets, fads, not valuing or understanding food. Said differently, "wimpy when it comes to food". The vegetarian, to the majority of the French, is someone who doesn't take food seriously. Well, I understand food. I love it and what it means, particularly in France when it goes beyond ritual and tradition. *La table* in France signifies so much more than just "the table". It means a place where family and friends can eat, drink, talk and be together, often for hours, over a simple, fresh meal. But I also value each individual life and especially in the case of factory farming, foie gras and other undeniably cruel practices. I no longer believe a few minutes, or even hours, of my pleasure is worth an animal's life, or suffering…What difference is there between my dog sitting next to me in a Parisian restaurant and the duck or lamb on my plate into which I'm about to stick my fork?…

We are all in this together, and helping the animals doesn't preclude us from helping humans. In fact, showing compassion to those supposedly weaker than us may be the first real step of social progress. As Gandhi said, "The greatness of a nation and its moral progress can be judged by the way its animals are treated." Compassion, like love, is such that the more you give, be it to humans or to animals, the more you have.

## No Debate

*Zarinea Lee Zolivea was interested in vegetarianism as a child, but it was a yogi, a chicken and a giant marlin who helped her live true to her beliefs.*

From the time I can remember, I felt extremely close to animals. I never enjoyed eating meat, but did not understand why. From childhood through early adulthood, several pivotal and traumatic situations occurred in my life that marked my decision not to eat animal flesh. The first event occurred when I was seven years old, one day when my mother had just served breakfast. I asked my father what we were eating, and he said that we were eating a cow. I was horrified. It was incomprehensible to me how an innocent animal could be killed, cut up, and sold for food. I told my father I no longer wanted to eat meat, but he said I had to. He then proceeded to explain the importance of eating meat. Something told me this was inhumane. I knew that when I was old enough to make my own decisions, I would choose otherwise.

Time passed, and my father taught me to like the flavor of steaks, but I still despised the idea of killing animals. Then when I was seventeen years of age, while taking a summer business course, I walked into a business bookstore to purchase my textbook. As I reached up to pick out the book, an invisible hand stretched up further, and in so doing, I saw a book titled *Yoga for Americans* by Indri Devi. I knew that I was destined to read it, so I purchased the only copy I saw, and subsequently stayed up all night reading this wonderful book. It still amazes me how this book ended up in a business bookstore. The author taught me that over 50% of the world's population is vegetarian. I knew then I would follow suit when time gave me the privilege.

The opportunity finally came during my three year stay on the lovely multi-cultural island of Singapore. It was here that another crucial event took place. I had gone to the town square market to buy chicken. Instead of purchasing chicken packaged in cellophane, the consumer had to choose a live chicken, who was then decapitated and her feathers removed. The corpse was then cut up and ready for sale. After witnessing this suffering, I decided not to purchase any chicken. This event affected me greatly.

While in Singapore I had the privilege of taking yoga lessons, an experience that influenced me to study Hinduism and Buddhism. Many life lessons were learned, most importantly, to respect life in all forms.

Thereafter, I discontinued eating meat for the most part, except fish. However, this changed one summer when I visited the beautiful island of Catalina, where I witnessed the killing of a giant marlin. The fisherman was acclaimed a hero for catching "it"—him or her—but I wept at the sight. It occurred to me that this being must have had feelings. Sure enough, just a few years ago, a scientific study was conducted on marine life proving that indeed these creatures are sentient beings, with a pain system that functions like that of human beings.

After my daughters and I left Singapore, we continued to eat mostly vegetarian. Then about five years later, while at a church retreat, we made the decision to become full-fledged vegetarians. It was tough for us at first, as we were not acquainted with anyone else who followed our philosophy. It was very difficult for my parents, as they did not understand our beliefs. However, my stepmother tried her best to prepare vegetarian meals when she invited us over for dinner.

Another significant occurrence happened in 1987 when *Diet for a New America* by John Robbins was published. Based upon eight years of research, including collaboration with over 20,000 doctors throughout the world, the book impressed me greatly. Robbins taught me about the horrors of factory farming, how our food choices affect the environment, and how many diseases are caused by the consumption of meat and dairy products. His book enabled me to make the transition from vegetarianism to veganism.

Robbins also influenced my profession when I was an instructor at an adult secondary-education school in Claremont, California. One of the subjects I taught was nutrition. I was able to teach both philosophies, that of the textbook and that of veganism, and I introduced the work of both Robbins and Dr. Michael Klaper. When the students were asked to debate both issues they said, "There is no debate." Spirit had helped me to teach them as well as humanly possible. Naturally I was delighted at their abundant enlightenment.

This commitment, the best choice I have ever made, has had a profound effect on my life. I am concerned about the suffering of animals, the violence perpetrated upon them, the assault on the environment, and world hunger. All these evils are lessened a little as a result of my choices. In addition, my health has improved and my body feels lighter.

It appears to me that this is an avenue for bringing in more light, as George Fox, the founder of the Society of Friends, feels is paramount. Since I have adopted Quakerism as a way of life, my existence is now so much more joyful. The values that are set forth by George Fox are those I have held deeply all of my life. For example, Quakers do not believe in war or in hierarchy, but in manifesting peace and social justice. This is what life is all about, both in our relationship to our fellow humans and to animals. My heart is grateful to Fox. His inspirational writings and his indomitable spirit have inspired me to look for "The Light" in all sentient beings.

My intensive pilgrimage journey continues, in the words of Keats, as a "Season of mists and mellow fruitfulness". My prayer and hope is that all human beings will not only walk in the light, but also come to an understanding that all life has meaning, and should be respected.

*Zolivea, Zarinea Lee. Online Vegetarian Friends journal.*
*"The Peaceable Table", December, 2005, vegetarianfriends.net.*

# CHAPTER SIX

# Laying Down Their Guns and Hooks

*They say that the battle is over*
*Finally the war is all won.*
*Go tell it to those with the wind in their nose*
*Who run from the sound of a gun...*
John Denver

Hunters and fishermen often have a knowledge of animals rarely known by the majority of human beings. They are witnesses to the magic and majesty of animals who are free. We have known many men and a few women who hunt and fish, and many have told us that they love and respect the animals they kill. They love the outdoors and the adventure that accompanies the hunt and the camaraderie.

Yet, at the very foundation of their relationship with the animals they hunt, there is an assumption of dominance and an unquestioned right to kill them with weapons against which no animal can defend him or herself. Their knowledge is applied toward destroying the life of the animals they hunt rather than toward appreciating our kinship with them.

Imagine a human hunter with no weapons. He would be more prey than predator. Without the claws, fangs, teeth, and sheer strength of a carnivore, human beings are completely vulnerable. We *Homo sapiens* have spent centuries living in fear and, for that reason, inventing powerful weapons and machines of death and destruction in an effort to protect ourselves from what we perceive to be a dangerous world.

As Matthew Scully, former speech writer for President George W. Bush stated in his book *Dominion*, "[Animals'] lives entail enough frights and tribulations without the modern fire-makers, now armed with perfected, inescapable weapons...It is our fellow creatures' lot in the universe, the place assigned them in creation, to be completely at our mercy, the fiercest wolf or tiger defenseless against the most cowardly man. And to me it has always seemed not only ungenerous and shabby but a kind of supreme snobbery to deal cavalierly with them, as if their little share of the earth's happiness and grief were inconsequential, [and] meaningless..."

The stories in this chapter show just how far hunters and fishers must travel in consciousness in order to stop the killing. By coming to the conclusion that their actions are killing not only the animal, but also their own souls, they must face their complicity in this violent industry. Memories surface of the innocent and helpless creatures they have killed. It is not an easy path to travel, but, as we will see, it is a path that has led them to a place of inner peace and deep connection to the wonders of nature that formerly eluded them. From hunting to animal protection is a giant leap, but for these men, it was worth the effort.

## Dog Bites and Wake-up Calls

*Ken Damro is the author of* A Northwoodsman's Guide to Everyday Compassion. *He is among the many hunters who finally saw the true essence and innocence of the animals they were hunting and stopped, never to hunt again. The universe brought Ken many surprising messengers ranging from a dog, a deer, and a baseball player to bring him to his present place of peace and compassion.*

My transformation from a carnivore/omnivore to my present "vegan" status is not a story of past tense. In fact, since no human (that I'm aware of) on earth today is a perfect vegan, then we are all at a point in our personal journey toward true veganism. Having said this, let me tell you about a transformation I went through—a transformation from a heavy meat eater and killer of animals to one who lives with more awareness and compassion today.

I had been an avid hunter and fisherman ever since I was old enough to carry a fishing rod and 410 gauge shotgun. Back then, I hunted mostly small game: squirrel, pheasant, grouse and most of all, rabbits. Rabbit hunting with beagle hounds was a multi-generational right for the males in our family. When I turned eighteen years old, I decided to move to Wisconsin's North woods where there was more public land to hunt and a larger variety of lakes and rivers to fish. When I say I was an avid hunter and fisherman, what I really mean to say is that I was addicted. Throughout many years of this addiction, I became quite "skilled", quite deadly; bagging more than my share of fish and game. One fine Sunday I was out afield with Mollie, one of my fine beagles, when she was caught in a steel foot hold trap. She cried and yelped fitfully, so I hustled up the small bluff to help her. The moment I bent down to help, she latched onto my shin with her sharp canines, mirroring the force of the trap itself. It was about the worst dog bite I'd ever had, and from my own mild tempered dog no less.

After that incident, I began to think that maybe my dog biting me was the Universe's way of proclaiming justice; after all, I'd trapped animals myself when I was younger. I began to wonder that if the Universe is just, what might happen to me in exchange for all the fish and animals I'd hunted and killed over the years?

I believe the trap incident was the first in a long string of events that eventually led to my quitting hunting and fishing. As years went on, I somehow knew that hunting and fishing were wrong, but I remained addicted. Like a drug addict, I'd sneak out to my favorite hunting haunts with my hunting clothes stashed away in the trunk of my car—just in case I'd run into someone I knew or in case I'd have to stop and run errands along the way. I didn't want to be associated with hunters and fishers anymore.

Because we Americans watch so much drama on the electronic screen these days, we have this notion that life changing events come along with intense music and/or narration. But as I get along in years, I find that real life transformation is often silent—or at least as silent as a beating heart. For instance, one fine summer's day, my wife and I were at a small town softball game hanging out with friends; drinking barley suds and downing a few hot dogs. All at once there was a base hit—a ball player slid into third base. In an instant he lay with his leg elevated—he had broken his ankle and all that was holding his foot from dropping to the ground was his long baseball sock. His bare broken bone protruded out the bottom of his pant leg like a beacon of pain. The crowd freaked out—people threw up and sobbed. Yes, on this day there was drama, and though there was no orchestra music playing, a life transformation was occurring.

I stood on my feet watching the entire scene—the puking fans, the ball player in distress—his team mates freaking out. All I could think about was how similar this ball player looked to a wounded rabbit. Often when hunting, I would shoot at rabbits as they ran through the underbrush ahead of my baying beagle hounds. Sometimes my lead shot would break one (or—gasp—both) of their legs, and they'd run for hours ahead of the hounds on a broken stub—a foot dragging behind as if it was attached to the rabbit's leg by a stubborn strand of baseball sock.

At that point, as I stood on the ballpark bleachers, there was no separation between the suffering of mankind and the rest of the animal kingdom. For the first time in my life, the concept of oneness had bolstered its way into my psyche. I never shot a small game animal after that weird August ball game.

Our state game managers would like to have us believe that if we weren't all out hunting animals, that these "game" animals would overpopulate the landscape and we would all suffer some dreaded consequence. For many years I fell for that unfounded line of reasoning and even after the ball game incident I continued to hunt deer based on the "game management" excuse. Then one day during a November deer hunting season, despite my best efforts for a clean shot, I wounded a doe. I gut shot her just before dark and had to leave the blood trail and resume tracking the next morning. Something happened to me while tracking that wounded deer in the early hours of the next day. I could see where this deer had bedded down in a pool of blood and intestinal bile—where its pain must have been so intense that it could no longer go on. But the most moving aspect of this scenario was that this doe had a companion—a deer whose hoof print was the same size as the doe I was tracking. Perhaps it was a twin, or just a close friend, but in either case, this deer stopped and waited for the wounded deer. I could see that the companion deer never left the wounded deer's side until it finally fell to its death. The entire time I tracked this pair of deer, I felt at least a portion of this deer's pain and distress. My stomach hurt, my legs felt heavy, and at times I felt weak, as if I had a bad flu. When I found the deer lying dead on the banks of a small river, I knew that it was the end for me. Like a drug addict who overdoses, hits the bottom, and finally gets sent to counseling, I knew I would never hunt animals again.

Throughout this personal journey, I was also a small livestock farmer. That's right—in addition to killing hundreds or perhaps thousands of wildlife, I also killed thousands of domestic animals. I guess it's no surprise then that my retiring from livestock farming came about in unison with my retiring from hunting and fishing.

I remember, about the time I was going through this personal journey, a serial killer by the name of Jeffery Dahmer from Milwaukee, Wisconsin, was apprehended. In an interview with Dahmer, he explained that among the reasons for killing his victims, was that of love and control. I remember him saying something to the effect that he loved them and didn't want them to leave him so he killed them; and in killing them, he was in control.

I thought then, as I do today, that most hunters, fisher people, and trappers kill innocent animals out of love and control. This is a possessive love—an immature love—a Jeffery Dahmer kind of love. I remember considering that either Jeffery Dahmer should have been set free, or perhaps every hunter, fisher person, and trapper who kills out of anything other than absolute necessity, should be behind bars with him—or at least engaged in intensive counseling.

In defense of these consumptive activities, as well as in defense of livestock farming, folks often tell me that if every effort is made to "use" all the parts of the killed animal, then this somehow justifies the action. And again, when I hear this I think of Mr. Dahmer, who also made such an attempt to use his victim's body parts for food, in the creation of furniture, a spiritual shrine, etc. Dahmer also admitted that eating his victims gave him special attributes—those of his victims. I have been around the hunting and fishing communities long enough to know that many of these "outdoorsmen" believe in similar myths, i.e. eating strong animals will make you strong.

I know drawing parallels between serial killers and hunters, fishers, and trappers can sound harsh to those who draw definite lines between humans and the rest of the animal kingdom. However, as time goes on, and as humanity continues its long awakening from the dark ages, it will become apparent that purposely killing sentient life of any species is a crime. And when this golden age of awakening arrives, then too, humanity will enjoy life without wars, starvation, widespread illness, and the lion's share of societal madness and un-justness that we experience today.

We as a human community desperately need to identify the cause of human insanity—that which lures us to both love and control— that which lures us into believing we are separate from others. In order for humanity to advance, we fully need to encourage mature love—that which is non-controlling, pure, compassionate, and altruistic.

## Why I Quit Hunting

*Roy Dallas Gragg had to question many family traditions in order to make a complete turnabout in his life.*

I was born in the mountains of North Carolina near Grandfather Mountain and Mt. Mitchell. Hunting, killing and butchering animals was a way of life for the mountain people. I killed my first hog at age eight. I had expected the animal to fall as if by magic when I squeezed the trigger of my grandfather's old .22 caliber rifle. I was both surprised and alarmed when the animal screamed with pain and agony. "More carefully," my uncle said, "You have to hit him in the head." When the rifle cracked the second time, the animal fell dead.

I couldn't sleep that night—I could still hear the animal's screams. The adults laughed the next day when I told them it just didn't seem right to shoot an animal when he was locked helplessly in a pen.

I dreaded October each year—that was the month when the hogs and steers were killed and butchered. Early in the morning barrels of water were heated over roaring fires to scald the animals so that their hair could be scraped off. I got a sick feeling in the pit of my stomach when a butcher knife slashed the hog's throat and the blood ran across the ground as the pitiful animal convulsed and kicked. The air smelled of death, especially when the hogs were gutted. I noticed that the horse, a huge Clydesdale mare named Bell, would sniff the air, and with big eyes run away. She too smelled the death. I always stayed outside whenever possible because the stench of lard being boiled on the woodstove was unbearable.

However, it was always my job to turn the handle of the hand-operated sausage machine. Spring brought another dreaded time, when the man came to castrate the pigs and dehorn the cattle. I would hold my ears to shut out the sound of their agonized screams. "Don't be a sissy—you'll get used to it," I was told, but I never did.

Sundays usually brought another unpleasant task: catching a chicken and "wringing" its neck. The sight of the unfortunate creatures' bodies jumping high in the air with a broken neck is still fresh in my mind, even though it was over thirty years ago.

To make matters worse, the butchered birds and animals had often been pets. I had a pet chicken named Red. I trained Red, a big red hen, to sit patiently on a fence post or other object for hours until I set her down. I also had a pet turkey named Fred. As is the fate of most turkeys, Fred ended up on the Thanksgiving table. The crowd roared with laughter when I said, "I'm not thankful. Fred was my friend and I'm not going to eat him." My cousins taunted me until I finally ate a small piece of breast, but I felt like a cannibal.

I rather enjoyed hunting because I didn't have to butcher the birds and animals. By the time I was fourteen I was a "crack shot". I never missed. Squirrel hunting was my favorite because the elusive gray squirrels were hard to hit. One day I grazed a big gray squirrel and he fell right in front of my dog Rex. The squirrel was putting up a furious battle against the dog who was many times its size. I sat down and thought for awhile. I couldn't help but admire the little animal. He had wanted to live!

The mountain people often shot the red squirrels or "boomers" for shooting practice. The red squirrels were not good to eat so they were thrown away. But that didn't sit right with me either. I doubted that God made his boomers just to shoot at.

One morning, as I sat on top of a steep hill waiting for the sun to come up and the game to start moving about, I noticed many small oak trees on the hill. Acorns are heavy, especially this variety. They were as big as chestnuts and probably weighed several ounces. I hadn't seen this particular variety before.

I strolled down the hill and crossed a small valley to another hill and found the parent tree, a huge oak about four feet in diameter. I was puzzled. How did the acorns travel across a valley to another hill? The wind didn't blow them, that was for sure, and floodwaters don't run uphill. I saw something move out of the corner of my eye. It was a gray squirrel leaping from a huge oak heading across the valley. I dropped the squirrel with a single shot. Imagine my surprise when I picked up the squirrel and he had one of those huge acorns lodged in his mouth! I had been shooting the planters of the forests! On the way home I said to myself, "So that's why God made squirrels."

A few years later, I joined the army and became qualified as an expert rifleman. "I have never seen anyone shoot like that," I overheard the sergeant tell the lieutenant. "He dropped sixteen men (targets) in less than twenty seconds!" Later the lieutenant said to me "You could do that in Vietnam, too. The slant-eyes are just bigger game." But I didn't make it to Vietnam. An ulcer got me a medical discharge and I returned home to the mountains.

I still hunted some but I thought about the squirrels. If they were nature's planters, what were the other animals' jobs? Later I noticed holly bushes in sheltered mountain valleys, over twenty miles from their natural growing range. It was quite obvious that birds had carried the seeds this great distance.

By the time I was thirty I had quit hunting entirely and began studying the birds and animals. I read books on ecology and the environment. And I returned to the forests—this time with a camera instead of a gun. I watched the squirrels carefully. They would always follow the same path through the trees, swinging like trapeze artists. Occasionally I would see a flying squirrel gliding silently through the trees or a ruffled grouse blasting away like a rocket.

I marked the spots where the nuts carried by squirrels fell and returned in the spring to find small trees growing in those areas. I also observed the "worthless" red squirrels burying nuts. It occurred to me that nut-bearing trees, oaks, hickories, walnuts, chestnuts and many, many others all depended on the little animals to transport their seed throughout the forests.

It should be obvious to any thinking person that nature is a powerful but delicate force. Each living thing on the planet is striving for survival in one way or another, and striving to keep its kind from becoming extinct. Various species of plants, birds and animals have survived earthquakes, tornadoes, hurricanes, fires, floods and many other kinds of natural catastrophes only to fall victim to uncaring humans.

Hunters are directly responsible—to name a few—for the extinction of the passenger pigeon as well as many kinds of island-dwelling birds. The buffalo very nearly became extinct after hunters [retained by commercial interests] went after them largely to wipe out the Indians' [main] food supply. Starve 'em to submission.

This strategy left more than 50 million of the great creatures on the plains to decay in the sun. Hunters have brought the mountain lion, the grizzly bear, the whooping crane, and even the symbol of our nation, the bald eagle, to the brink of extinction.

I began studying hunters from "the other side of the fence". When working with hunters, I would ask their opinions of hunting. One hunter's reply was, "God made animals for me to eat—what else are they good for?" Another said, "It makes me forget my troubles to hunt and fish." I thought long and hard about his statement. Humans vent their stress and their frustrations from daily life on innocent wildlife. Hunting is a one-sided game with only one winner—human beings. This is why hunters refer to birds and animals as "game". When the hunter has hunted down and killed an animal, he has "won" the game. More often than not, the creature is killed for pleasure instead of for food. A certain sadistic pleasure is derived by killing another creature. When a human kills an animal the act fuels his ego: he has mastered the creature by taking its life.

Why else would a trophy hunter spend thousands of dollars, hike through steaming snake and insect-infested swamps or climb steep cliffs to kill a magnificent member of another species? Why else would he cut off the head of his victim and leave the body to rot? Why else would he take the head to a taxidermist and mount it over his fireplace? He has dominated and killed the "beast", and therefore hangs its head up for all the world to see that he is the mighty and fearless hunter. It is nothing but fuel for the insecure ego of small men.

The hunter, with the scent of death in his nostrils, has little respect for his neighbor who enjoys seeing the creatures on his property alive. "No hunting" and "No trespassing" signs are torn down or shot full of holes. A hunting license is a permit to kill indiscriminately. Our government sells out our wildlife for the price of a hunting license. Soon after becoming an anti-hunting advocate, I found my tame mallard ducks shot and floating on their pond. They too had enjoyed living and I enjoyed them. But some pervert found pleasure in their death. Once I observed hunters exterminating a covey of Bob White quail. Their cheerful calls can no longer be heard around the small mountain community where I grew up as a child.

Tradition is perhaps the worst enemy of the animals: even our holidays call for the killing of birds and animals. These barbaric traditions, including hunting, rodeos and other cruel sports, are taught to children and thus passed down from generation to generation. Only a little more than a century ago blacks were considered to be animals and were treated as such. Similarly, during the second World War, Jews were considered to be subhuman by the Nazis, or perhaps even subanimal, and were killed by the millions.

Even today we abuse our fellow humans through boxing, wrestling and other cruel sports. How can the perpetrators of cruelty among us be expected to respect animals when they do not even respect humans? Before we can understand animal abuse we must understand ourselves. Humanity lives not by reality but by habits —often anchored in selfishness and staggering ignorance. It is this aspect of human nature we must work against.

If my story can, in some small way, influence the traditional way of thinking and the ignorant beliefs about our fellow creatures, I would be greatly pleased. This story is to aid our fellow creatures who have long suffered at the hands of mankind. May they someday live in peace, without suffering and fear.

*Gragg, Roy Dallas. Cyrano's Journal Online, found at bestcyrano.org.*

## The Hunter's Poem
Written by Lemuel T. Ward (1896–1984)

*We don't know if Mr. Ward was vegan, but we were so moved
by this poem we felt it should be shared.*

A hunter shot at a flock of geese
That flew within his reach.
Two were stopped in their rapid flight
And fell on the sandy beach.

The male bird lay at the water's edge
And just before he died
He faintly called to his wounded mate
And she dragged herself to his side.

She bent her head and crooned to him
In a way distressed and wild
Caressing her one and only mate
As a mother would a child.

Then covering him with her broken wing
And gasping with failing breath
She laid her head against his breast
A feeble honk…then death.

This story is true though crudely told,
I was the man in this case.
I stood knee deep in snow and cold
And the hot tears burned my face.

I buried the birds in the sand where they lay
Wrapped in my hunting coat
And I threw my gun and belt in the bay
When I crossed in the open boat.

Hunters will call me a right poor sport
And scoff at the thing I did.
But that day something broke in my heart
And shoot again? God forbid!

## I Was a Killer

*Steve Hindi, after hunting and fishing for most of his life, experienced a transformation when he witnessed a live pigeon shooting event. From that point on, compassion and vegetarianism, not killing, became his life goal. Steve founded an organization known as Showing Animals Respect and Kindness (sharkonline.org) as a vehicle for the protection of all animals. Steve, like so many other animal activists, constantly exposes and protests canned hunts, rodeos, bull fighting, and many other forms of cruelty. As a result, Steve has been incarcerated on many occasions in spite of the fact that he was legally exercising his freedom of speech and assembly. Here is Steve's story.*

I first fished at age five, with my brother Greg, who is one year younger. Each of us caught a perch out of a lake in St. Paul, Minnesota. Fascinated, we watched the two perch swim around in a small bucket until first one and then the other died. I don't remember what happened to their bodies, but I know they were not large enough to eat. Perch are plentiful, and easy to hook, and are therefore considered to be a good species for practice fishing. Many members from both sides of my family were fishers, as well as hunters, trappers, and ranchers. A couple of dead perch didn't rate much concern. Like most children, we learned what we were taught, setting aside whatever qualms we may have felt.

Our mother raised us to care for cats and dogs, and we regularly took in strays, despite housing project rules which forbade it. However, we were told that fish had no feelings, and we killed them with abandon. Our first decade or so were spent pursuing panfish, as they were prevalent around the lakes we were able to walk to. Sometimes family members and friends drove us to other lakes. On a good day we would fill up buckets or stringers of sunfish, crappies, bullheads and perch. Sometimes they were eaten, and sometimes they were simply thrown away. The most important thing was the acquisition: the victory.

In our early teens we also fished for carp. Although they are considered a "trash" species, not recognized as "game", they are much larger and fight much harder. Carp typically were left to suffocate on the shore. We were told this was good for the other fish in the lake, as carp supposedly turned the bottom to mud. Sometimes I would give a fleeting thought to whether these animals suffered as they lay gasping on the shore. Like catfish and bullheads, carp take a long time to suffocate. After a while, we would hit carps' heads with rocks to kill them quickly. Once we brought M-80 firecrackers to the lake. We stuffed one into the gill of a large carp, lit the waterproof fuse, and released him. Seconds later the water erupted in a red spray. When the muddy water cleared, we saw the carp's head, blasted away from his body. I watched tentacles of flesh sway back and forth in the current. Small fish inspected them with curiosity. For some reason we felt bad about this, although no one said anything in particular. We did not do that again. Looking back at it, however, I guess that victim suffered far less than those who suffocated.

In our late teens we got our own cars, and turned our attention to different lakes and larger game fish—trout, bass, walleyes and northern pike. Of these, northerns were my favorite, because of their aggressive nature. Often we bought large sucker minnows as bait. The suckers were hooked just under and to the rear of the dorsal fin, in a way that would allow as much movement as possible, and would maximize their survival time. Some fishers would run the hook through their eyes. The suckers were thrown out and suspended under a bobber, or were held close to the bottom by a lead sinker. The bobber was big enough to prevent the minnow from pulling it underwater, but small enough to be taken down by a larger predator as it grabbed the minnow. Although we were told, and wanted to believe, that fish did not feel fear or pain, we almost always knew when a predator approached the sucker. The bobber would begin to bounce and move; although the sucker wasn't big enough to sink the bobber, his or her panic was obvious. The bobber jerked, pulsed, and slowly dragged across the water as the bigger fish approached. Often the predator would only strike the sucker and let go, probably sensing that something was wrong. We would reel the smaller fish in to find him, or her, often still alive but ripped to shreds.

At one point I decided that live bait fishing was cruel and not particularly "sporting", and I pursued my prey thereafter with artificial lures or dead bait. This, I felt, would be more humane. As time went on, we increasingly often addressed matters of ethics and conservation, at least superficially. Spokespeople for fishing began talking of catch-and-release. This, they assured, would secure both the future of our victims, and the tradition of humans harassing and killing them. In catch-and-release, we would hook our prey, allow them to suffer as they fought for their lives, and then release them, hoping they would survive to endure this torture again. What we never bothered to admit was that any supposed quest for food, our supposed primary objective as hunters, played no part in our new ethic.

Yet we could not admit that the vast majority of us were pulling hooks into the mouths, eyes, tongues, throats and internal organs of animals simply because we loved the feeling of their struggle against our cruelty. At about the same time catch-and-release became popular, there came another move to make fish abuse more "sporting". This time the ethical gurus decided that fishers should use lighter gear to fight our victims. It was of course no accident that the move spawned a whole new avenue for profit. There were smaller reels, lighter lines, and lighter rods made of new materials. New record classifications were developed that gave almost anyone a chance to hold a "world record" because he or she killed a weird-size fish with some weird-class line. Fishing magazines taught anglers new methods to use with ultra-light gear. For me, ultra-light methods were a very successful method of destroying many species of fish.

Of course, using ultra-light gear condemned our victims to more suffering than ever in the name of sportsmanship. We thought it was great. A small fish could be fought not for a couple minutes, but perhaps for a quarter of an hour, half an hour, or more. As someone who invested heavily in ultra-light gear, I was able to in some cases extend my victims' misery for hours. I even wrote articles on the subject that appeared in local fishing magazines. Coming of age, as I reached my early twenties, I continued my quest for bigger fish. One goal was to catch a fish over forty pounds. For a midwestern freshwater fisher, this was not easy. Few midwestern freshwater species ever top forty pounds. I wanted either a muskie or a chinook salmon, and for a few years spent plenty of time, effort, and money in both U.S. and Canadian waters, searching for my trophy. When I wasn't fishing, I was either working to make the money I needed to pursue fish, planning my next expedition, or reading up on my obsession. A library book about shark fishing almost immediately convinced me to try it. Over the next few months, I made ready for a trip to the Atlantic Ocean.

At first, my conversion to shark fishing seemed to quell a fairly quiet but nagging voice suggesting that killing animals, especially those much smaller than me, was not completely defensible as a hobby. Many fish species are under incredible pressure from humans, but I told myself, as sport fishers still tell themselves, that commercial fishers do the real damage. Commercial fishers, of course, claim the opposite. In truth, there is a fine, often indistinguishable line between the two factions. We are all guilty, though few who still fish will admit it. In the spring of 1985 I drove to Montauk Point, Long Island, New York. I immediately found that my preparations were completely inadequate. Nevertheless, by a stroke of luck and macho stupidity, I succeeded in killing a seven-and-a-half foot, 230-pound mako shark, despite my undersized boat and equipment. My fish story about the one who didn't get away was written up in the *New York Daily News.*

For the next few years I heard my story retold by those who did not know I was the human participant, and it was a real ego boost. Fishermen love to tell stories, whether their own or someone else's.

Every year, the fish became larger and the boat became smaller. In truth, I had ambushed a fish who was merely seeking a meal, and subjected him to five hours of agony before killing him. For some years the mounted shark hung as a trophy on my office wall.

At home were other mounted animal bodies, testimony to my insecurity, insensitivity, and willingness to kill for fun. As I look back, the whole thing seems quite macabre. Over the next few years I went to the ocean at least twice a year, for two or three weeks at a time. I bought a new boat, made for ocean fishing, and named it the One Resolve, because of my determination to hunt and kill a rare thousand-plus-pound great white shark.

I stole the lives of uncounted victims of many species. But what should have been a killer's dream come true was somehow losing its luster over time and death. On occasion we would go night fishing for tuna offshore. Tuna are large, very strong fish, with rigid bodies. Once pulled onto the deck of the boat, they beat their tails incredibly fast and furiously. They can break a fisherman's foot. When the bite was on, the deck could literally be full of tuna struggling for life. In order to keep them still, we simply put a cloth over their exposed eye to block the light and calm them, much as you would calm a horse. This was a problem. Much like a horse? How much like a horse? I wouldn't do this to a horse. Why was I doing this? For years, I managed not to answer that question.

There was also the time that sea birds were bothering our lines in the chum slick. A chum slick is a gooey mixture of ground-up fish, dumped into the water to attract sharks. It also attracts birds, who swoop down to pick at bits and pieces of fish. Sometimes birds would hit our lines, or temporarily get their feet caught in the line. One day when the sharks weren't biting, that was more than I was willing to tolerate. One bird was particularly bold, and refused to react to yells, waves or anything else I did to dissuade him. So I shot him. At that close range, he was dead immediately. His body upended, and his legs flailed. While my logical mind knew he was gone, my conscience told me that I had done something rotten, and to finish it. But the shotgun jammed. The next thirty seconds seemed like thirty minutes as the bird's legs kicked and "ran", and slowly came to a halt. It was almost half an hour before his body floated out of sight. I watched almost the entire time, knowing I was the world's biggest asshole, trying desperately and unsuccessfully to convince myself that I had a good reason to do it.

Then my brother and I encountered a baby mako shark next to the boat, in our chum slick. Mako sharks are fearsome-looking, with large gnarly teeth and coal-black eyes that make them look as if always enraged. But this miniature version, of about twenty pounds, was just plain cute, like a lion cub trying to strut his stuff with baby growls and tiny hops, feigning attack. My brother Greg asked if he could catch the baby, and have him mounted. This was a common practice, but one that I abhorred. This was, after all, a baby. From a fisher's view, however, he was also a lot cheaper to mount, and did not require the room a large fish did to display. Initially I refused to allow the capture, but when the baby hung around to gorge on the chum, a sorry version of brotherly love won out. No effort at all was required to capture the baby. Greg stuck a dead hooked mackerel in front of him, he grabbed it, was hooked, and Greg swung him into the boat, into a fish hold. We did not shoot or even hit the baby in the head: that would ruin the mount.

I don't remember how long it took him to die, but it was very long. Every now and then I would open the hatch to see if he was dead yet, and he would look at me. Sharks can move their eyes to a point, and they can and do follow activities around them. I will never forget that baby watching me as I waited for him to die. This was probably the lowest I dropped in my long history of killing. Then came the day that a friend and I hooked into the largest mako shark I ever saw. She looked like an ICBM missile when she jumped, and my friend and I were so fearful that our legs shook. This was going to be the trophy of our lives. For the next two hours we fought and fought just to get the huge animal close to the boat. But a short time after the fish began the familiar circling around the boat that indicated the start of fatigue, the hook pulled out. Probably she had been "foul hooked", meaning hooked in the body somewhere other than the mouth.

Our dreams of a "monster kill" were shattered. We fished the area for the rest of our trip, but without ever so much as seeing our "trophy" again. When we were ready to leave for home, we were still sulking like scolded puppies. I moaned and groaned my disappointment to the marina manager, with whom I had become good friends. His response was not what I expected. He looked me in the eye and said, "Steve, I'm glad you didn't kill that fish"..I was so taken aback, I said nothing. He told me that such a large mako was almost certainly a female. He said he recently learned that females had to attain many hundreds of pounds before even reaching the age of giving birth. With the mako population in serious decline, he said, we had to stop killing them. This made sense to me, even if I still wanted that "trophy". But then he said, "I'll tell you the truth, I just don't know how much more of this killing I can take." Oh shit. Now that nagging voice I was hearing for years wasn't just in the back of my mind any more. It was being voiced right in front me, by a friend. I didn't know what to say, except to murmur that I respected his right to his opinion. I didn't say that I was having a tougher and tougher time trying to deny this feeling in myself.

One of the last straws occurred at a most odd time. I was fishing with a friend and working companion named Rick, with whom I had taken a number of successful fishing trips in the past. We hooked a 200-pound mako shark right at the end of the day. The fish jumped repeatedly and fought hard, all of which we should have enjoyed immensely. Having brought the victim to the side of the boat, I made a good shot with my .357 magnum revolver, right on top of his head, resulting in an instant kill. Rick and I brought our victim right up next to the boat, and as was customary, I sank my hunting knife right behind his head to sever the spinal cord. This insured that sharks, who are very tenacious of life, were truly dead. As the beautiful luminescent blue of the mako began to turn gray with death, I turned to Rick and said, "You know, I just don't enjoy this the way I used to." There. I had said it. That nagging feeling that had dogged me for so long now had a voice, and was my own. But things got stranger when Rick, his smile disappearing, said, "You know, I feel the same way." What was my world coming to?

I don't know how long I might have been able to ignore my observance that I was doing something indefensible. It might have gone on for years. Fortunately, Hegins, Pennsylvania lay close to the route I took from Chicago to Montauk. On the way to my boat in 1989, I chose to stop and see the infamous Hegins Labor Day pigeon shoot. After witnessing my first pigeon shoot, my perception of my animal trophies was never the same. But I did not quit killing easily. Initially, it never crossed my mind that I would actually stop doing what I had done for three decades. My intention was to stop these vile pigeon shoots, and then go on with the vile things I was doing. I approached many of my hunting and fishing friends for help in fighting pigeon shoots, which as I explained, were not only unethical, but cast all of us "legitimate sportsmen" in a bad light.

With the exception of my brother, none of the great hunting "conservationists" were willing to take any time away from killing to actually try to help animals. It was about a year before I gave up blood sports. God knows how I fought to continue to kill. Leaving blood sports meant accepting a whole new set of values, and eventually coming to terms with owing a debt I could never repay. But after Hegins, it became clear that I would have to try. Greg and I buried our "trophy" victims, including my first shark and the baby mako, in a grave on our family property, next to the graves of beloved nonhuman family members. I donated the One Resolve to the Sea Shepherd Conservation Society.

As I tearfully bade her good-bye, I renamed her the New Resolve, for she would now be used to save lives instead of taking them, to rescue marine animals in trouble, and to patrol for poachers. A few years later, we would even be briefly reunited on the coast of California, while trying to stop Chicago's Shedd Aquarium from capturing dolphins. When I first talked to activists about fishing, at Hegins in 1989, one person asked me, "Would you still fish if they had vocal cords?" I believe the answer in most cases would be no. Fishing is as popular as it is precisely because fish do not have the ability to communicate suffering as readily as cats, dogs, cows, or other mammals. But I know they suffer tremendously, just as we would if subjected to such horrendous treatment. While many people may at first be taken aback at the mere suggestion that fish can suffer, I believe society can grasp the concept. And if we can make people feel for those who cannot cry out their suffering, how much more will they feel for those who can?

After the Hegins incident, something reached down into my heart and soul that I could not bury or ignore. A deep empathy for the animals who cry out in agony and pain at being exploited and victimized—a sort of "calling" for me to expose right from wrong—I had to "do" something to make their lives better, to stop this insanity against our fellow beings. Don't get me wrong, I still have the "hunter mentality", but I am hunting a different species, and this time my weapon is my camera.

Taking care to never cross over to the "dark side", SHARK exposes —to the public on film, and in the boardroom—the brutal abusers that believe it is their "right" to use, exploit and harm animals as they please. This method has stopped some serious inhumane canned hunts, rodeos and bullfights. Now when they see us coming with camera and crew—they know a change is coming. They are going to have to be accountable for their actions and either change them, or be haunted and exposed in every media outlet available to us and resulting, in some cases, in shutting them down.

I live my life as an animal defender, with the "Golden Rule" as my signpost.

*This story was first published in* Animal People, May, 1996.

# CHAPTER SEVEN

# From Slaughter to Salvation

*When a human kills an animal for food,*
*he is neglecting his own hunger for justice...*
*Even in the worm that crawls on the earth there glows a divine spark.*
*When you slaughter a creature, you slaughter God.*
Isaac Bashevis Singer, 1978 Nobel Prize Winner

Slaughterhouse workers—how do they do it? Day in and day out, taking lives, watching innocent animals suffer, doing tasks that no one on this earth should ever have to perform. How do they function on a day to day basis? It *has* to affect them. It affected a man named Virgil Butler, who became a vegetarian after his experience.

In testimony given via PETA in January 2003, Virgil Butler documented the horrific treatment of chickens that he witnessed every night while working at the Tyson chicken slaughterhouse in Grannis, Arkansas from 1997 to 2002. His testimony and ongoing website revelations resulted in a front-page article in the *Los Angeles Times* on December 8, 2003, "A Killing Floor Chronicle". On August 21, 2004, at United Poultry Concerns' (upc-online.org) 5th Annual Forum in Norfolk, Virginia, Virgil gave his first conference presentation about his Tyson experience, "Inside Tyson's Hell—Why I Got Out of the Chicken Slaughtering Business".

"I worked on the back dock, where I hung live chickens in the shackles and worked the kill floor. I was lead hanger for the last few years, so it was also my job to teach new-hires how to hang and kill chickens. In the hanging cage, I stood on a line with six other guys where we took live chickens off the belt and hung them by their legs upside down in the metal shackles. The line goes by at about 182-186 birds per minute, so a hanger must be able to hang 26-30 birds per minute. As lead hanger, it was also my job to catch the empty shackles that the new-hires would miss. I spent so much time catching empty shackles and one-leggers (birds hung by only one leg), that I didn't have much time to train anybody to do anything."

He adds, "...the way the chickens hang there and look at you while they are bleeding trying to hide their head from you by sticking it under the wing of the chicken next to them. They were trying to hang on to every last bit of life they could. Bless their souls.

"Some nights I worked in the kill room. The killer slits the throats of the chickens that the killing machine misses. You stand there with a very sharp 6-inch knife and catch as many birds as you can that the machine misses because the ones you miss go straight into the scalder alive. You have to cut both carotid arteries and the jugular vein for the chicken to die and bleed out before hitting the scalder. This requires quite a bit of skill and entails quite a bit of risk. It's the most dangerous job in that department. All but one of the most serious accidents I saw the whole time I worked for Tyson, occurred in the kill room due to the killer having to cut the throat of a one-legger. Some of those accidents happened to me. I have scars all over my hands from working the kill floor.

"The killing room was worse than the hanging cage. It really does something to your mind when you stand there in all that blood, killing so many times, over and over again. The blood can get deep enough to go over the top of a 9-inch set of rubber boots—I have seen blood clots so big that it took three big men to push them. You have to stomp them to break them up to get them to go down the drain. That can happen in just two and a half hours. We filled up a diesel tanker truck with blood every night in one shift. I have actually had to wipe blood clots out of my eyes. Working as a killer was what I hated the most. But since I was good at it, that was where I got sent a good bit of the time."

*Reprinted with permission from Karen Davis: " 'Slaughterhouse Worker Turned Activist': UPC Talks with Virgil Butler and Laura Alexander".* Poultry Press, *Fall 2004, Volume 14, No. 3.*

In a video interview with *Compassion over Killing* (cok.net) Virgil stated, "The cruelty I witnessed by the other slaughterhouse workers was horrific." He adds, "I saw people stomp chickens to death; throw chickens against the wall; pull their heads off; throw them in the dead pile—alive; run over them with forklifts; I've seen chickens frozen to the belt and frozen to the sides of cages. If you can imagine it, and it's horrible, I've seen it happen."

Virgil stated further that one of the most powerful things that happened to him was making eye contact with the chickens on the slaughter line and seeing the terror in their eyes. That never left him.

Virgil Butler died on December 15th, 2006, leaving behind Laura, his life partner, and pages and pages of journals. You can read more about Virgil at cyberactivist.blogspot.com.

Bless Virgil Butler for speaking out for the animals.

## The Decision

*Laurie Crawford Stone worked in a slaughterhouse in Iowa with her two brothers. This experience had a profound effect on each of their lives and, as we shall see, on what they now choose to eat.*

It was during the 1970s that Laurie worked at a slaughterhouse in the human resources division. Her brothers Dave and Bruce also worked there. Part of her job required her to walk through the area where the animals were being killed. "The first time I appeared on the 'kill' floor," recalled Laurie, "an employee threw a cow's tongue at me as I stared horrified at the cows being stunned..." She also witnessed hogs running and trying to escape from their certain death. "Their screaming is a sound I will never forget."

While working there she noticed that many employees spent breaks at a bar near the slaughterhouse to try to forget and, as she put it, "to numb themselves for their afternoon's work". She was also witness to the area where injured animals known as downers (because they could not walk) were left outside in all kinds of weather to suffer and die. Although injured and often sick, they were eventually dragged to the rendering area. "The clothing I wore on visits to this area was thrown away when I left the slaughterhouse for good. The stench could not be washed away."

After leaving her slaughterhouse job, Laurie became a vegetarian, as did her brothers. Dave is now vegan. Laurie made it clear that she became vegetarian (and is moving toward veganism) for ethical reasons, not for her health, although her health has greatly benefited. The kill floor experience convinced her to never again take part in causing such suffering.

*Stone, Laurie Crawford. "The Decision", from Sharon and Daniel Towns' (ed.) book* Voices from the Garden: Stories of Becoming a Vegetarian. *New York: Lantern Books, 2001, pp. 145-147. Retold and quoted with permission from Lantern Books.*

## The Butcher

*After 25 years of killing animals in slaughterhouses, one day Peter Raz-pet-Petko of Slovenia experienced an intense spiritual change which made him put down his butcher's knife forever. Peter told his deeply moving story in this interview with the All Creatures.org organization.*

Q: How do you remember your childhood and youth?

*Peter:* Ever since I was little I have been incredibly fond of animals. I used to bring home puppy dogs, only a few days old, rejected by other people. I liked feeding rabbits, pigeons and squirrels. Later at school I had little success, because I felt I didn't need such an education. So when I was in the sixth class I already applied for a job in some local company. At that time we had a bull. My father once beat him up. That is why the bull started to hate him, so my father did not dare to come close to him anymore. I used to talk to the bull a lot and caress him. But every time my father came into the stable, the animal started to fret and fume, so he finally decided to sell him. Therefore we took him to the cattle market in Cerkno. The butchers from Idrija bought him, but couldn't get him on their truck. He obeyed only me. However, I can still see tears in his eyes when I tied him to the truck and said good-bye. When the butchers saw how the bull followed me without any resistance, they offered me a job in the slaughterhouse. I actually don't know why I had accepted their offer. The next week I started to work there. I shall never forget my first day in the slaughterhouse. They cut off the heads of twenty fully conscious calves right there in front of me. I felt like throwing up and could not imagine me having to do it. A young cleaner noticed my disgust and said: "There's nothing to it, boy. If I can kill an animal as a woman, it will be much easier for you as a man!" Then she took an ax and hit a living cow with it. Something broke inside of me and I said to myself: "Well, O.K then, I'll be a butcher."

Q: How do you explain your decision for a butcher's job?

*Peter*: I am sure there are no coincidences in life. Obviously I had to pass such a bloody way. The bull with tears in his eyes surely wanted to warn me, but I did not understand the message at the time. As a teenager I simply did not understand, that God created people, animals and plants in this world to learn from each other. And I really still do not quite understand why I had killed the animals, which I liked the most for so many years. However, it seems a bigger mistake to me, if you are aware of doing something wrong. In this case spiritual law of sowing and harvesting is even more inexorable. I really wasn't aware that slaughtering animals was wrong up to that moment.

Q: Do you regret your decision?

*Peter*: No, not at all. All things, that seem negative to us, have their positive side in a wider spiritual perspective. Every man has to experience darkness, before he can recognize brightness and love. Therefore we mustn't judge anyone. My opinion is that Jesus and Hitler had a similar role. Jesus wanted to teach us how to love, forgive and be kind. I am sure that Hitler on the other side wanted to teach us something we shouldn't do. In my younger days I caused quite a lot of troubles, so my father often spanked me in an old farmer way. I couldn't understand why I liked him so much, even though he beat me up once in a while. Only when I had my own kids and once wanted to spank my daughter, I remembered in a flash, how my father's strokes hurt me. I became grateful to him only then, because I suddenly realized what he had tried to teach me: Do not beat the one you love! Every man becomes aware, why he is sent to this world and starts to live a completely different life. When I was a butcher, I simply didn't notice the beauties and wonders of nature, God and all the universe.

Q: But you must have slaughtered very unwillingly all those years?

*Peter*: I think that unwilling slaughterers are mostly butchers who had been forced into this profession by their fathers. Every man has free will and I don't see how some parents can force their kids to do certain jobs. Although my father was a village butcher all his life, he never expressed a wish for me to do the same job too. I think I always made reconciliation with an animal before killing it. I did not kill with hatred. Father and I used to slaughter pigs in villages and killing days with pork and sausages were always a kind of holiday for village people. But I repeat, at that time I never thought of a pig as a victim of our enjoyment and revelry. On the contrary, it was the pig's death itself which joined us. I could agree with older village people who once claimed: No matter how bad their relations were, birth or death always brought them together.

Q: What does a slaughterhouse look like?

Peter: I'll say this: Slovenian societies for animal rights should organize visits to slaughterhouses so many people could see how their steaks get on their plates. I am sure most of them would soon stop eating meat. Most meat eaters would resist in disgust, if they were told their puppies would be slaughtered. But most of them really don't care what goes on behind the walls of slaughterhouses.

Q: How do animals behave before their cruel death?

Peter: Thank God, I wasn't aware of it at that time. Nowadays, whenever I think of what I have been through, I remember many things. How the animals resisted me just like our bull had resisted those butchers when he didn't want to get on the truck. I could write a book of memories. I remember tears in the eyes of the calves I had slaughtered. But I tell you once again, thank God I did not always see it, let alone understand it. I am sure of one thing: If nowadays I asked a cow or a bull if I could kill him, he would give me some kind of a sign not to do it. Killing or taking someone's life to appease hunger or thirst is not a sin, but it is a mistake which will have to be rectified by individuals as well as by humanity. I am lucky, I don't have to make similar mistakes anymore.

Q: What do butchers do with slaughter waste?

*Peter*: Once we used to bury all slaughter waste, horns, intestines, eyes and bones into a special hole. Nowadays they use all that for the production of feeding stuff, which is the main disaster. This also causes many terrible diseases. Besides that, they add many chemicals to meat in order to preserve durability. Some of the chemicals cause cancer. Some pieces of meat, which should be wasted, are remade to salami or hot dogs.

Q: What happened? What made you quit the job of a butcher?

*Peter*: One day four years ago a relative of mine suggested that I should visit a fortune teller in Zasavje. I felt she might know something because everything she said about me was true. Then she threw cards on the table and found out I knew many people, but the job I was doing was completely wrong. I told her not to talk rubbish and bid farewell. I was busy buying a slaughterhouse at the time. I had a lot of money and was quite sure of my success, so her words didn't make sense to me. At parting she was sure I would visit her again.

Q: What happened then?

*Peter*: Troubles in my business really soon began. Many business partners didn't pay me, so I soon ran into debts myself. Besides, my home folks turned their backs on me too. In great distress I took refuge in praying to God. Then I started visiting Brezje regularly. Once, when I was really desperate, I prayed to Mary Mother of God and begged her to give me power of forgiving. Instead I heard a clear voice: Do not kill! From that moment on I kept to my promise. A few days later, at the end of the year, I was at a birthday party with my friends. I was the only one not eating meat, ignoring their remarks, what kind of a butcher would I be if I didn't eat meat.

Q: What was happening to you in the next few days?

*Peter*: I began praying to Mary to save me from all those nightmares and help me, because people didn't understand my new way. I know, many people didn't get my point then, so after my hospitalization I went to Father Leopold in Brezje, who is incited in Mary's miracles. In a conversation which lasted more than an hour, I confidentially described to him all the events that had recently happened to me. He assured me that after all humiliation and suffering my decision not to kill animals brought me God's grace, although he didn't quite understand how. But he warned me to keep my experiences to myself as much as it is possible, because people would not understand me and I might have troubles again. He added that miracles happened every day, we just didn't notice them anymore in our heartless, materialistic world. My wife didn't understand all the events. She was sure I was sick. That is why I remembered Jesus saying: If you really believe and trust in me and God, just stand up and leave. I often asked myself where, but there was no answer. I found the answer in me only when I really did it. I got a divorce, left home leaving everything to my wife and kids.

Q: How did you feel physically?

*Peter*: After the change (going vegan) many people said I would get sick not eating meat because of certain vitamin deficiencies. Passing on to vegetarian food I became lighter, more active and had much more life energy. I could say, my subconscious and consciousness began to act completely differently. Many people thought I was sick, but in fact I had never felt better in my life. I gave up all medicines prescribed to me in the hospital. When I told that to my doctors after a year and a half asking them for explanation, they remained speechless. If people knew how much poison they take with every medicine, they would reconsider carefully before taking it. I wonder why people don't ask themselves how our predecessors managed to live to be very old not knowing any medicines except the natural ones. It is interesting how I used to despise vegetarians.

Q: Did you notice any more positive changes after quitting the bloody job?

*Peter*: I haven't hated a living being ever since I decided to start a new life. Above all I remember my puppy dog Pika. She was so glad, because I had changed and from that day on we have never parted. When we were strolling along the countryside, I noticed gratefulness in her eyes, which many people couldn't understand. She often comforted me when I was in distress and clinged to me when I was down.

Q: Do you ever feel tempted to slaughter an animal?

*Peter*: No, not at all. Nowadays I cannot even kill a fly, because it also has the right to live. As I said, I like all the creation. My evening prayer is: I send my love to all people, my brothers and sisters and to all the creation given to us by God, who said: Love each other.

Q: The Church is still saying that God's Commandment—Thou shall not kill—refers to people only. How do you comment on that?

*Peter*: I know an ex-priest and religious historian, who was in service in Rome for a few years. He told me he ate more meat there than in his whole life. The Church doesn't really care for its own commandment: You shall not kill! The bloodiest wars humanity has ever known raged and are still raging in the world in the name of religion or because of it. How can we expect this commandment to refer to animals, if it doesn't refer to people? If the commandment was respected by everyone, the world would need neither priests nor state or religious leaders, because everything would go on according to natural laws which are unfailing and eternal. As the Church and its leaders as well as the leaders of the world do not want to obey this commandment due to their benefits and manipulation with people, I can hardly believe that killing would soon be over. However, I do believe that God's and natural laws are strong enough and that there are people in this world, including priests, who are getting more aware every day. With their help we will slowly change the world to what it used to be from the very beginning. Evil was created by man, not God, therefore we will have to eliminate it by ourselves, for it was caused by us. Anyway, after the change I realized that people really didn't need altars and churches, where priests often manipulate with people. A proverb says: God will not ask you how many times you attended masses, he will be interested in your acts. Faith in God is not enough, it is necessary to be active. God himself will not do anything. We will have to unroot evil by ourselves.

Q: What do you do nowadays?

*Peter*: I established a society to help people in distress. In many different ways I help people who got into trouble. Having experienced many hard times, I can understand them and help them in different ways. I dedicated myself to nature and I live with it, so I also started to gather medicinal herbs. I heal with the help of bio-energy. In this way I treated many diseases which couldn't be healed by official medicine. I also work on my spiritual development and using my own experiences I help people who were pushed into distress by a modern way of life and are searching for new ways. I am also active on the cultural field. But I am most thankful to God for sending me to this world right now to accomplish all these things. I experienced a lot of beautiful, unforgettable moments. I accepted all the tests as my destiny, fought them and won. Help yourself and God will help you, is one of the most truthful proverbs. I enjoy very much various handicraft skills too. I like making all kinds of products, chapels among other things. I especially cherish the Christmas time. Every year I make a big crib in memory of my new way. Together with God and Mary I can experience the birth of Jesus, whom we can see in every living being and nature, if we wish so.

Q: Tolstoy said that people would kill each other as long as there were slaughterhouses. How do you comment on his statement?

*Peter*: I will say a little differently: Blood will be shed until man becomes aware that God created animals to be friends. Not only animal blood, but man's as well. First we have to raise the spiritual consciousness, then slaughterhouses will automatically disappear from the earth. People will not eat meat anymore, therefore it will not be necessary to kill animals and destroy nature as well as everything that was given to us by God as a present.

## The Smell of Death

*As told by Judy*

Several activists and I were downtown one warm, summer night with a portable TV showing a film called *Meet Your Meat*, about the way farm animals are raised and killed. It wasn't easy to watch. We were putting glass walls on the slaughterhouses by showing what goes on inside them. One group of macho college guys stopped and proceeded to declare that it was all fake. "They don't treat animals like that," they claimed. "PETA just makes that stuff up"..

Just as I was about to open my mouth, a big, burly guy who had been standing there watching for a while, began to speak. In a loud, no-nonsense voice, he said to the group of laughing men, "No, you're looking at exactly how it is in slaughterhouses. Mostly, it's a lot worse than that." Not to be dissuaded, one of the men challenged him by asking how he could possibly know that. "I worked at the IBP slaughterhouse in Emporia, Kansas, for too many years," he said. "I've seen it all—the most horrible suffering you can ever imagine. And what's really terrible is that the workers get so messed up by the endless violence that they laugh, like you are laughing, at the live cows kicking and mooing as their legs are cut off."

When I asked him how it came about that he stopped working there, he told me that one day, he suddenly realized he wasn't laughing along with the other guys. It was as if something inside him had awakened and he saw the horror of what they all were doing to these innocent, defenseless cows. He was overwhelmed by the dark and heavy energy field of violence and suffering that permeated the entire place. And that energy field finally got so heavy and powerful that it forced him into a new consciousness. He left the slaughter-house that day and never returned. He became vegan overnight, and the dark energy began to lift.

As a little follow-up to this story, the slaughterhouse where he worked closed in 2007. It will be a meat packaging plant, but no lon-ger will 4,000 cows a day be driven to their deaths in that building that was drenched in blood for so many years. While there will still be an aura of darkness and misery hanging over the plant and affect-ing the town, the energy field will not be quite as dense and heavy as it once was. This is bound to have an effect on the crime level and general well-being of the town. We shall see.

Not long after this encounter, I met another man who had worked at the same slaughterhouse. I asked him how it affected him. "The smell of death was everywhere," he said. "I quit after a week. I'd rather starve than eat an animal now."

> For hundreds of thousands of years the stew in the pot
> has brewed hatred and resentment that is difficult to stop.
> If you wish to know why there are disasters of armies
> and weapons in the world, listen to the piteous cries
> from the slaughter house at midnight.
> Ancient Chinese verse

# From Farmers to Liberators

*What do they know—all those scholars, all those philosophers,*
*all the leaders of the world—about such as you? They have*
*convinced themselves that man, the worst transgressor of all the*
*species, is the crown of creation. All other creatures were created*
*merely to provide him with food, pelts, to be tormented, exterminated.*
*In relation to them, all people are Nazis; for the animals it is an*
*eternal Treblinka.  And yet man demands compassion from heaven.*
Isaac Bashevis Singer, 1978 Nobel Prize Winner

Farmers and ranchers, like the hunters in Chapter Six, experience what they consider a sort of love for their animals. However, as ex-hunter Ken Damro so aptly put it, it is a love based on control. It is a love that always leads to the suffering and death of the animals in question. Certainly none of us would want to be loved in that way.

For anyone who wishes to explore the origins of animal agriculture and how it has led to human overpopulation, starvation, subjugation of women, war, deforestation, 10,000 years of patriarchy, slavery, pollution, and worldwide suffering beyond imagination, Jim Mason's *An Unnatural Order* and Will Tuttle's *World Peace Diet* will explain the process well. These books make it clear that animal agriculture is one of the most massive and tangled roots of human and animal misery, and until we dig up that root and expose it to the light, we are in for more of the same. The stories in this chapter come from three animal agriculturalists who saw the damage that they and humanity were doing and made up their minds to help eliminate the cause of all the pain.

What is so affirming and hopeful is that, in liberating their animal brothers and sisters from suffering and certain death, they themselves have found a liberation of spirit that they had never known before.

In 1992 Cesar Chavez, the great social justice activist for farmworkers and others received a Lifetime Achievement Award from the organization In Defense of Animals. In his remarks he said "We need, in a special way, to work twice as hard to help people understand that the animals are fellow creatures, that we must protect them and love them as we love ourselves...We know we cannot be kind to animals until we stop exploiting them...in the name of science...in the name of sport...and in the name of food."

## The Mad Cowboy

*Howard Lyman is the author of* Mad Cowboy *and* No More Bull—*a fourth generation cattle rancher and now vegan. Howard is best known as a guest on the* Oprah Winfrey Show, *and for the lawsuit that ensued between Cactus Feeders and Howard and Oprah. The two of them endured and won the six-year-long trial. Howard travels over 100,000 miles per year speaking and teaching about compassion and vegan living. How does a rancher whose livelihood depends on cattle and whose friends laugh at vegetarians, do a complete turnabout and still find peace? Here is Howard's story.*

As a fourth-generation family farmer in Montana for almost forty years, I speak from a background of personal experience when I say that chemically based agricultural production methods today are unsustainable, and therefore ecologically disastrous. My experiences range from working in a large organic dairy to raising registered beef cattle to owning a large factory feedlot. I have farmed thousands of acres of grain and reproduced a herd of over one thousand commercial beef cows. In addition to raising cows, I have raised chickens, pigs, and turkeys. I have also grown crops such as wheat, barley, oats, corn, alfalfa, and grass.

I was involved in agriculture at a time when the call dictated getting bigger and better or getting out. I was educated in modern agriculture, and I can tell you from firsthand experience—it is not sustainable. I followed all the modern advice and turned a small organic family farm into a large corporate chemical farm with a thousand range cows, five thousand head of cattle in a factory feedlot, thousands of acres of crops, and as many as thirty employees. I saw the organic soil go from a living, productive base to a sterile, chemical-saturated, mono-cultural ground produced by my so-called modern methods.

In 1979, a tumor on my spinal cord caused me to be paralyzed from the waist down. That changed my life forever. I promised myself that, whatever the outcome of the surgery, I would dedicate the rest of my life to doing what I believed to be right—no matter what changes that necessitated.

The period before and after the surgery gave me much time to think about the changes resulting from my methods of farming. Convinced that we were going the wrong way, I decided to become a voice for the family farmer and the land. In 1983, I sold most of my farm and started working for farmers in financial trouble. This led to my working for the Montana Farmers Union and from there to Washington, D.C. as a lobbyist for the National Farmers Union.

For five years I worked on Capitol Hill for America's family farmers. In that time we had some small successes, such as passing the National Organic Standards Act. But even after the act became a law, it took the administration several years to allow funds for its implementation. I became convinced that the changes needed had to come from the producer and the consumers at the grassroots level. Until that alliance is put into play, the big money interest will continue to control public policy in the Congress of the United States.

The question we must ask ourselves as a culture is whether we want to embrace the change that must come, or resist it. Are we so attached to the dietary fallacies with which we were raised, so afraid to counter the arbitrary laws of eating taught to us in childhood by our misinformed parents, that we cannot alter the course they set us on, even if it leads to our own ruin? Does the prospect of standing apart or encountering ridicule scare us even from saving ourselves?

That prospect intimidated me once, and I can only wonder now what I was frightened of. It's hard to imagine, now that I'm a hundred thirty pounds lighter, infinitely healthier, more full of life and energy, much happier. Now that I have vegetarian friends wherever I go, and feel part of a movement that is not so much political as it is a march of the human heart. Now that I understand how much is at stake. Now that I've come to relish shaking people up.

I would love to see the meat industry and the pesticide industry shaken up, too. I would love to see feedlots close and factory farming end. I would love to see more families return to the land, grow crops for our own species, and raise them organically. I would love to see farm communities revive. I would love to know that I've wandered into my nation's heartland by the sweet smell of grain and not the forbidding smell of excrement.

When you can't take it with you, all that really matters is what you leave behind.

I would love that all the animals that have been killed would know that I'm working on stopping the killing of all species. I just want to be the poster boy of unconditional love on planet earth.

## Snickers' Nudge

*Harold Brown spent half his life farming and was raised on a cattle ranch in Michigan. For the past seventeen years he has been vegan after initially changing his diet due to high blood pressure and a family history of heart disease. At the time he didn't even know what the words vegetarian or vegan meant. He actually learned about the word from a bumper sticker on the back of a car that he repaired. The slogan read, "I don't eat my friends." He recently founded FarmKind.org. Read how a loving cow named Snickers gave Harold one of the greatest gifts anyone could hope for.*

In my long journey from growing up on a predominately beef farm (we also raised rabbits, pigs, and dairy cattle), I grew up with an indoctrination to how animals ranked in the hierarchy of the cycle of life. I also hunted.

Indoctrination is defined as: "to inculcate (to teach or impress thoroughly), to instruct". In other words, it involves being given information that one does not examine critically. My relationship to farm animals and free living animals began with, of course, my family, then my community, church, 4-H, a land-grant college and then was reinforced every time I turned on the TV. Every commercial break has at least one commercial that is selling flesh, dairy, or egg products and if they are inventive they can cram all of them into one sandwich. Back then, when I saw this I thought that what I was doing was a good thing, providing food for the family and others.

It wasn't till I had a health crisis that I looked seriously at the cause and effect of my lifestyle choices. I had a heart attack when I was eighteen years old. At the time, I didn't know what had happened. I was home alone while the family was on vacation. I was sitting in front of the boob tube watching a movie and eating a half-gallon of ice cream. All of a sudden the left side of my neck started to hurt, then my left jaw, shoulder, and a radiating pain down my left arm. The next thing I knew I was on the floor and couldn't breathe. It seemed to last forever, but I now realize it probably lasted only a few minutes. The experience scared me. I didn't know what had happened. I didn't know the symptoms of a heart attack. It scared me enough to not tell my family about it.

A few years later my dad had a heart attack and by-pass surgery. I then learned what a heart attack really was. This caused me some concern, but, being young and invincible, I figured it couldn't really happen again. But when the cardiologist met with my dad, brother and myself in ICU step-down we were told that we had a genetic predisposition to heart disease.

Again, being a person who followed the cause and effect line of thinking, I watched and followed the advice given my dad—no smoking (never did that), take the salt shaker off the table, and keep my saturated fat intake to 30% of total calories. My dad followed the guidelines and a few years later had another heart attack and his second by-pass. Later he had a stroke that took his ability to speak and after that an abdominal aneurysm that nearly killed him. It took several years for all of this to play out.

There is an old saying, "Either your life is an outstanding example or a terrible warning." The warnings were all around me. Lifestyle choices had caused serious health problems and death in my family, but I didn't know better.

In the late 1980s I was working in the dairy industry. I injured myself on the job, and, since we were unionized, I went to the union doctor. He fixed me up and then asked me how long it had been since I had had a physical. It had been about ten years so he gave me a complete physical and also a full panel blood test. A few days later he called me and said we needed to meet. It wasn't something he wanted to discuss over the phone. When a doctor says something like this, you know it can't be good.

I went to his office, and he asked if there was a history of heart disease in the family. I said "yes" and explained what had happened to my grandfather and my dad. He had my dad's attending physician fax over my father's preoperative blood work. He sat there studying and comparing. Needless to say his furrowed brow and occasional expressions of "hmmm" and "I see" were making me nervous. These little signals never bode well.

After several minutes he flatly stated that, if I didn't make some changes in my lifestyle I would probably have my own by-pass by the time I was 35. I asked him what to do, and he handed me a pamphlet. It was about heart health and, as we discussed it, he said that the number one food I had to get out of my diet was ice cream. Yikes! I was addicted to ice cream! The pamphlet said to start by giving up ice cream and red meat. It didn't suggest being a vegetarian at all. Besides I wouldn't have known what the word meant. Never heard it before.

I took the pamphlet home and my wife and I stood in the kitchen and read and discussed it. She said that we could make the transition together, bless her heart. So we did.

About a year later we moved to Cleveland, Ohio. It was there that I learned what a vegetarian was and that I could reverse my heart disease with diet and exercise.

We joined a local vegetarian club and developed close friendships with some very amazing people. Through their mentoring and my reading everything I could get my hands on about the relationship of diet and disease I became a vegetarian and, a year later, a vegan. After reading and meeting doctors like Dr. Caldwell Esselstyn (earthattackproof.com) and Dr. Michael Greger (drgreger.org) who specialize in reversing heart disease and other diseases I realized that, if I was going to create homeostasis in this thing I call a body, then the responsibility is totally upon me. Not a pill or surgical procedure but upon the choices I make every time I eat. I find it interesting that all physicians have to take the Hippocratic oath when they graduate but know so little about the teachings of Hippocrates. One of Hippocrates prime teachings was "Let food be thy medicine and medicine be thy food." Good advice!

A few years later I began to gain what some call animal consciousness. That is, I became aware of how my food and lifestyle choices were affecting animals. If you watch the Tribe of Heart documentary *Peaceable Kingdom: The Journey Home*, you will see me talking about how this came about.

In the film, you will see me explaining how Snickers, a Guernsey steer, changed my life forever. It is hard for me to describe such an emotional event, and you can see in *Peaceable Kingdom* that I have to choke back my tears just to explain it. I had met Snickers at a sanctuary for rescued farm animals. As part of their fundraising, the sanctuary encouraged visitors to "adopt" a specific animal by helping to pay for their food and care. I chose Snickers to adopt and then returned some time later to visit him again.

I was standing at a distance from him when he saw me. It was as if he knew I had adopted him and cared about him, because he came straight over to me, and placed his big furry head right against my chest, right where my heart is, and just pressed against me for the longest time. And that's how I was awakened and transformed at the very deepest soul level—by Snickers. He touched my heart and opened it with his innocence and gentleness.

Through this experience, I realized how, in my past, I had developed coping mechanisms that allowed me to view animals as objects of utility. I had an immediate image in my head of a light switch over my heart that I could turn on or off depending on who or what I was dealing with. I also realized that the cue for that coping mechanism was the phrase "I don't care." I now understood that, when I made a choice that was not in alignment with my authentic self, out of tune with my heart, I would say "I don't care," and uttering it would put me in a place where I was disconnected emotionally, and even spiritually from "the other". In that moment with Snickers I knew that I could no longer be part of anything that took a life and that I could never use that phrase again. What I learned then was that, if I choose not to say "I don't care," then I have no alternative but to say "I care." I will call it unconditional caring, but it might be better understood as unconditional compassion, and it has profoundly changed my life. It has required a tremendous amount of hard work to practice emotional honesty; something our culture does not teach folks and particularly males.

Make no mistake—I didn't take this journey alone. If it wasn't for my loving wife and an amazing community of friends in Cleveland, I may have not found the peace that I have today. The vegetarian club I joined in Cleveland consisted of people dedicated to personal growth and self-actualization. If they hadn't provided me with a safe space to explore the deep emotional traumas of my life I probably wouldn't have come to understand some very important truths.

One of these truths is the practice of ahimsa, doing no harm. Most people can understand this as karma, or in the West we say, "What goes around comes around." How we live our lives and the things that we do or don't do have everything to do with the reality we create. Since I was a kid I had observed that farm animals sought comfort, pleasure, good food, shelter, and community. But I never allowed those observations to trump the dominator culture that I lived in. When I allowed myself the moral imagination to include these animals into my moral universe it became clear that the most simple observations we make about animals we call pets are no different for farm animals. When I made the choice to live a conscious life, it demanded of me to question long-held assumptions. It also demanded that I think critically about what I had observed earlier in my life and to integrate the two opposing ideas.

Beyond these, more or less intellectual pursuits, was the harder task of coming to terms with how I truly felt. Emotional honesty was where the hard work would be. And so it has been. Not only is emotional honesty counter-intuitive to males in our culture but considered by many to be a sign of weakness. But in my heart of hearts I knew that this was where I needed to be, how I needed to show up in the world. And if I was to make any sort of difference for a better world I had to live this truth.

Animal rights, to me, is quite simply respecting animals as the sentient beings that they are. This means that they are on this earth for their own reasons, not ours. That they have their own self interests just as humans do and, in so much as they do, they should be respected for that and left alone.

But this is also the proverbial up hill battle animals face. They are the legal property of humans and this dynamic puts them at a grave disadvantage, in particular, in a free-market capitalist system where animals are owned and traded openly as commodities, as economic units. Until we question this entangled relationship, which has existed for some 10,000 years we will have some difficultly seeing animals with new eyes.

I think we innately know that this is not right (killing and eating animals). Otherwise, we wouldn't feel so bad about it. And if it was righteous, if it was a truly good thing, it would be a joyful thing. But I've never known anybody that slaughters animals that finds it a joyful thing. I'm not saying that I've got it all figured out. But I can tell you that I have greater peace in my life than I've ever had. And to me that's what life is about. I mean, at the core of every human being and every sentient being, all we want is peace. And love.

*Most of this essay by Harold is reprinted with his kind permission from his website at FarmKind.org/AR.htm.*

## The Vegan Cowboy:
## Nothing needs die that I might live!

*Thomas Rodgers calls himself the Vegan Cowboy, but in his earlier days, he would have laughed at such a title. It took a near death experience to awaken his compassion for all forms of life. Here and on his website (vegancowboy.org), he recounts the physical illnesses and trials that led to his transformation from cowboy to cow defender and spokesperson for health, compassion for all beings, and peace.*

My experience and belief is that in return for my restored health and renewed life, I must search, learn, know, then do what I have learned! Then I must sacrifice my personal comforts and time to labor, write, teach and share what I can to benefit others! This brief page is part of that sharing. My hope is that from this sharing, you will be encouraged, learn, and make beneficial change!

In February of 1990, I am with my wife Betty and daughter Cindy, just days before serious cancer detection, surgery and treatment work began. Far exceeding 250 pounds (I stopped getting on the scales out of self embarrassment and denial) and no longer feeling like I was the invincible, unstoppable, independent entrepreneur and functional man I had labored to be for decades. As my own boss in my some-times "animal husbandry" and all-the-time "mechanical" responsibility and business, I was never short on exercise. My work was always physically demanding and strenuous. I could "throw" a cow, "drop" a cantankerous horse, pull wire or break thread on the largest rusty pipe or bolt without difficulty. I did unfortunately believe—as I had been thoroughly taught—that I needed to "sufficiently" consume—for the "good" of my health, teeth and bones— the products of my own past dairy and animal husbandry industry. I had no shortage of milk, eggs or flesh! I should have been as healthy as my old horse, Frisky. But it was not so!

So while undergoing the heroic efforts of honorable VA and University physicians and staff—doing the very best they had been taught and intent to save my life—I suffered several TIA (strokes) associated with (or during) two cancer surgeries each of over three hours. My life declined and its limits became no larger than the hospital ward or my own imprisoning bedroom. All else in my life's dreams and efforts collapsed, vanished or were taken.

In June 1990, after those first surgeries—a subsequent (3rd) stroke took my sight, and left me with little speech and motor (muscle) function impaired (fully on left side). Two and a half years of endless headache, pain and perpetual nausea was now in process! Depressed with my dysfunction, overwhelmed, as therapy (additional cancer cleanup surgeries) and treatment continued! My world no longer fully visible, workable and for the most part communicable, nor rational, crumbled about me. So, unannounced to me, as my oncologist, neurologists and internal physicians labored with my body, a team of psychiatrists were quietly adding to my cabinet full of practitioners and beneficiaries. And their tiny pills further disconnected me from logic and life.

By November 1990, continually sedated, irrational, and without help, my business and finances crumbled. It was in January 1991 that my heart was tired, damaged and wanting to stop. So I was sped again out of my own bedroom back to my old familiar emergency bed in the VA for an encounter now with another cold steel table in cardiology and more threats of additional surgery. This time on my heart! If I could survive my cancer! So yes, my life was returned, as usual and as before, back to my bedroom, but—with some more pills to take of course!

On June 30th my immune system had failed against a strep A infection and all systems did stop, as toxiplasma brought near fatal anaphylaxes! Though heroically salvaged by excellent dedicated men and women of the VA, I was still left blind—with struggled speech— endless headache and pain. Nausea and dysfunction were now amplified and continued. (A fourth stroke in September did follow.)

Passing near death, I understood nature's wisdom—and my foolish errors! I had to make and so did make compassionate intelligent change! Prior to June 29 1991, I would have consumed most anything placed before me. But on June 30, my struggled, and strangely out of character words, to the hospital dietitian—who I surprisingly requested to come to my side immediately as I was salvaged from death in that emergency room were: "Nothing need die, that I might live!" Sensing her and everyone's disbelief from this old once-rancher's request, struggling again to speak, I restated "Nothing is to lose its life, so that I may have mine!"

That wonderful lady of the kitchen facilities understood. And from that day forward—as my "angel" in the hospital kitchen—she made sure that my hospital menu was only of gentle foods!—that nothing more was to suffer for me!—or my appetite!

As a former dairyman/rancher, this new way of thinking was unusual, uncomfortable, even offensive to many of my friends and family; most—like me—with our dairy ranching roots, profits and pride set firm in the long honored (and lucrative) "traditions of our fathers!"

But Death's embrace did work profound change in my way of thinking! Never again to be the same!

The 5th day of April 1992 was once a (medically) predicted death date! But here I stood, sweetly living! 60 lbs lighter; sight, speech, and mobility returning; blood analysis equal to a twenty year old;

immune system back and working; remaining growth under rib reducing; third mass in groin—gone; arthritis, varicose veins (& hemorrhoids), tinnitus, etc. healing; teeth (what I had left) securing; even hair, its color and thickness returning!

But the most important healing for me was my returning ability to play and interact again with my children and family—and of course, with open hearted friends!

In September of 1992, I am wonderfully alive at 179 lbs and continually getting better—living on those compassionate foods that nature designed and has always meant to sustain human health. All my family members are now deleterious and dead foods free!

Twenty-four months after lying on a gurney and running towards my death, I was granted the joy of completing a 26.2 mile marathon in the desert.

Wise, compassionate living may not make me any more handsome, but it sure has brought me to friends of unmatched kindness, valor and visible beauty. What a happy honor to have at your side beautiful (and famous) friends who are now no longer "clueless" in caring for the precious temples of human spirit—and who are willing to speak out, and courageously *act* (literally) as "Warrior Princes" in defense of all the voiceless, helpless and innocent life of creation—including humanities' own priceless children—and for our one, and our only—and *not-replacable* earth.

So my prayer (now added to those of so many), is for an earth —where man, acting wholly in wisdom and peace, is healed—and learns creation's eternally facilitating truth specific to the nourishment and well being of the human frame!

That truth is consistent with real human physiology, honest science, my own wonderful experience and that of so many thousands more: "And when man has learned—and acted in this frame, then all creation will live—permitting Man the same!"

*This is a short version of Thomas Rodgers' story.*
*The complete version with photos can be found on his websites*
*tomrodgers.org and vegancowboy.org.*

# CHAPTER NINE

# Stories from Today's Youth

*Each second we live is a new and unique moment of the universe,*
*A moment that will never be again...And what do we teach our children?*
*We teach them that two and two make four, and that Paris is the capital*
*of France. When will we also teach them what they are?...You have*
*the capacity for anything. Yes, you are a marvel. And when you grow up,*
*can you then harm another who is, like you, a marvel? You must*
*work—we must all work—to make the world worthy of its children.*
Pablo Casals (1876–1973)

Awww, the young! So impressionable, innocent and so caring. I, Tina, cannot recall ever meeting a child who wasn't mesmerized by animals.

Many children I have come into contact with, once they had learned who was in the meal they were being fed, rebelled and would not eat it—just as I did. I refused to eat animals at a very early age, but unfortunately was forced to eat what was on my plate. Many times I placed the little pieces of flesh that I abhorred onto the floor under the dining room table for our dog to eat. I know many children who have used napkins, trips to the restroom, and other methods to discard the flesh they could not consume.

It really helps children if their parents acknowledge their refusal to eat flesh. I know our parents made us eat it and their parents as well. However, perhaps children know a little more than we do. I have always believed that children have a special inner guide that has not been tainted by modern technology, advertising, and other outside influences. Children can usually sense a person with bad intentions much more quickly than an adult can. Could it be that they are closer to the spirit of God, being so new on this earth?

Whatever the case, I think we can learn a lot from children.

### Karmic Resonance

*Jim Atherton is a good example of a child who knew at an early age that he did not want to eat meat. He was nine years old at the time. Here, at age eighteen, he tells us his story of how he became more healthy and spiritually fulfilled by becoming vegan.*

As a younger person, my period of transition to veganism was slightly difficult, in a family of somewhat conservative individuals. I had become a vegetarian at the age of nine, and around the age of sixteen became introduced to veganism through a close friend. Even though I had been confronted by "meat-eater's propaganda" about how vegans are "too thin", and "prone to illness", I was ready to make the step; I felt I needed to do my part to help stop the cruelty that my species impose on my animal friends. Instead of finding myself spiral into constant illness (and though my mother was increasingly worried about my health), I found myself feeling more healthy and spiritually fulfilled.

I found myself falling sick to common illnesses far less than my meat and animal-product eating friends. I found, in my teenage years, that my skin was much clearer after cutting dairy out of my diet.

Through veganism, I try to be more productive and life-bringing rather than destructive and life-taking. In turn, for me this reduces a sense of negative karmic resonance, and I can live my own life happier and more peacefully, knowing that I am not supporting an industry of mass cruelty.

In Lak'ech.[a Mayan greeting]

Jim Atherton, age 18

*This story came from the website veganrepresent.com.*

## The Slobbery Cap

*Connor Posey found a connection between the steak on his plate and the heifer who showed him her playful personality while he was working on his uncle's fence.*

When I was thirteen, I worked on my uncle's farm for two weeks. Although he does grow a lot of different stuff, most of the land is unmaintained and natural, which is pretty cool. He has a bunch of cows, probably about two dozen, that have hundreds of acres to themselves most of the year. He uses them to maintain different fields by eating the grass, and keep the soil rich with their manure, so compared to many cows, they have the life of a (cow) god. I had never really made the connection between the steak on my plate and the cows in the field. One was food, the other was a big, slobbering animal.

One of my jobs while on the farm was to remove old, rusty barbed wire fences that had been there for more than 50 years. That was quite a chore. One of the fences I had to eliminate was in the field that the cows were in. It was a big field, so they were about two or three miles away from me, way in the distance.

I was listening to music to take my mind off the extreme Texas heat. I listen to my music loud, as most teenagers do, so I could not hear anything going on around me. After about two hours of solid work, I sat down to take a drink, when all of a sudden my hat was taken off the top of my head. Figuring it was my uncle screwing around with me, I turned to grab it. I came face to face with a full grown heifer, with my cap in her mouth! The whole herd was around her, staring at me like I was going to give them something. I made eye contact with the heifer for probably fifteen seconds before reaching out my hand to get my hat back. She dropped it at my feet, looked back up at me and walked off with a deafening moo. The herd followed her lazily, swatting flies off their backs with their thin cow tails. I put the slobbery hat in my pocket, chuckled a little, and went back to work.

Later that night at my grandparents' house, we were having a dinner of steak, vegetables, and dinner rolls. My family is a religious one, so they pray before each meal. Since I am not religious, I usually stare at my food and wait for them to return to reality so I can chow down. But this time I just stared at the steak. I had now come into contact with what I was eating, I now knew that steaks and cows are, indeed, the exact same thing. On the other side of the living room, my hat was on the couch. It only took one look at that nasty, cud-stained hat to realize that I couldn't eat the piece of flesh in front of me. I then remembered times when I had come into contact with other farm animals, at petting zoos, farms, stock shows, and other places. I remembered a time when I was at a petting zoo and there was a pot-belly pig in a pen, sleeping in the mud. I walked over to it and poked it in the nose, as many children do. It snorted, woke up, and stumbled to its feet, and sniffed at my hand. I spent the rest of the time at the zoo with that pig, just watching it and becoming acquainted with its personality. But I was still too young to make the connection between that pig and the bacon I had for breakfast.

I remember one stock show I went to—there was an acre full of chickens. Chickens of all kinds, waddling around and plucking at random things in the dirt. I remember chasing one hen around, delighting at the way it moved its little legs. The hen had no interest in me, but it was an honestly fascinating creature, making the strangest sounds. Again, I was still too young to make the connection between that chicken and the McDonald's chicken nuggets I had for lunch that day.

All of this hit me right there while my family was praying. I told them I didn't feel well so I could get out of eating that death on my plate. I went to the bathroom and had a good sob. I thought that the feeling of guilty sadness every time I saw a piece of meat would fade quickly, but it didn't.

It took me about a year and a half to go vegan. My philosophy has changed drastically in the past year. It went from thinking meat was fine if the animals were treated humanely before the slaughter, to thinking that any form of animal abuse, exploitation, or cruelty is unacceptable with very, very few exceptions. I never want to be seen as a "vegan Nazi", but it is very hard to bite your tongue when someone treats you like some sort of freak simply because you are humane and healthy...But I digress.

My mother has always been supportive of everything I have taken an interest in, and veganism was no exception. She helps me cook vegan dishes, helps me shop vegan, and even altered her own diet to vegetarian. She is the only person in my family who thinks I am sane for what I do. My friends even think I am crazy.

*This story can also be seen on veganrepresent.com.*

## Animals Are My Friends

Alejandra Tumble does not eat meat, because she thinks it's wrong. She's ten years old.

Alejandra is one of 45 children who took part in a study of moral development conducted by Harvard doctoral student Karen Hussar. Hussar was aware that famed psychologists, Lawrence Kohlberg and Jean Piaget, had concluded that children were not capable of making independent moral decisions at such a young age.

However, Hussar and her advisor Professor Paul Harris, decided to explore the possibility that young children could indeed have a sense of morality. In deciding what sort of children to recruit for the study, Hussar suspected that vegetarian children would be ideal. She theorized that vegetarian children whose parents were meat eaters would be examples of children who, despite family pressure, stuck to what they believed to be right and moral. Likewise, those children who were from vegetarian homes would be contending with peer pressure to eat meat and would nevertheless hold to their values.

"When you talk to kids about bullying or teasing, they all know the right answers and can say it's wrong," said Hussar. Vegetarian children, on the other hand, do not have any such prescribed and generally accepted answers to the question "Why are you vegetarian?". Hussar's research and interviews found that all of the children made their decision to become vegetarian for moral reasons rather than for any personal benefit such as feeling healthier. "Their responses were more about how animals are their friends," explained Hussar.

Some of the responses of these children between the ages of six and ten included simply wanting to be nice, not wanting to kill animals and not wanting to eat them because they love them. Their responses certainly pointed to an ability to formulate a moral priority for themselves.

As Hussar continues to do her research on morality in young children, she will not only be amassing data supporting their early moral development, but also she will be helping to document a growing courage among children to question the dominant paradigm of abuse and destruction and choose a higher path, in many cases, entirely on their own.

*Anderson, Jill. "Why do young children choose to become vegetarians?",* Harvard Graduate School of Education News Features, *August 8, 2006. gse.harvard.edu/news.*

## Vegan for Life

*Sarina Farb, who is now fourteen years old, was born into a vegan family. She has never known the conflict and misgivings that so many children have felt who grew up in meat eating families. Here she tells us about her unique life growing up in a home dedicated, from the start, to nonviolence and lovingkindness.*

I have been vegan for as long as I can remember. It wasn't a conscious choice of mine in the beginning; it was just what our family did and had always done. It didn't really occur to me to really want to eat anything that wasn't vegan. Most of the time the friends we hung out with also ate the way we did. When we did go places and saw other people eating non-vegan things, my parents would talk to me about why we didn't eat that.

Some people argue that it's wrong to deprive children of the chance to eat meat and dairy. The way I feel is that it's wrong to not tell children what they're really eating. I think all children should be taught compassion in all actions they take including what they are eating, and when they get older then they can consciously choose what they want. When I was seven my parents gave me my own food choices and said that I could eat whatever I wanted. At this point it didn't even occur to me to eat meat since I never had and never really wanted to.

I am fourteen years old and now spend lots of time around friends and other people who are not vegan, and I still have no intentions of eating meat or anything that in any way harmed animals, ever. Being vegan means more than just a diet to me. It is a way of living compassionately and not harming animals or the planet. It is a system of ethics and morals. It is a way of life. Being vegan has made me more aware of all my choices and it causes me to think long and hard about what's really right.

For example at an outdoor camp last summer there was a big emphasis on kindness to nature and not messing with animals or disturbing their natural habitat. I thought this was wonderful. There was one thing that bothered me though. They also had catch-and-release fishing there. This disturbed be greatly because I could not see how it was ok to hook fish in the mouth, pull them out of their habitat and then throw them back in and yet it was NOT ok to touch or pick up the snakes and turtles and other creatures. I talked to several of the other kids and some of them chose to abstain from fishing with me.

I feel very blessed in many ways and very thankful to have been raised this way and taught to think for myself. It has never felt like I am being deprived or missing out. I feel that others are missing out on the chance to know that they are not contributing to animal suffering.

# CHAPTER TEN

# Animals and Religion

*That's all nonviolence is—organized love.*
Joan Baez

Many influential religious leaders, priests and saints have been advocates for animals. Some have also endorsed a vegetarian diet, arguing that since animals are God's creatures they have their own place in the universe and that it is wrong to kill.

As evidenced here, and later in this book, many religious writings comment on the need for compassion and consideration towards God's creatures in order to find a true connection to God.

**The Arakanga Sutra** is the first of the eleven Angas, part of the agamas (religious texts), which were compiled based on the Jain teachings of Lord Mahavira.

On ahimsa it states:

"I so pronounce that all the omniscients of all times, state, speak, propagate, and elaborate that nothing which breathes, which exists, which lives, or which has essence or potential of life, should be destroyed or ruled over, or subjugated, or harmed, or denied of its essence or potential. This truth, propagated by the self-knowing omniscients, after understanding all there is in the universe, is pure, undefileable, and eternal. In support of this Truth, I ask you a question—'Is sorrow or pain desirable to you?' If you say, 'Yes, it is,' it would be a lie. If you say, 'No, it is not' you will be expressing the truth. What I want to add to the truth expressed by you is that, as sorrow or pain is not desirable to you, so it is to all which breathe, exist, live or have any essence of life. To you and all, it is undesirable, and painful, and repugnant."

"That which you consider worth destroying is (like) yourself.

That which you consider worth disciplining is (like) yourself.

That which you consider worth subjugating is (like) yourself.

That which you consider worth killing is (like) yourself.

The result of actions by you has to be borne by you,

so do not destroy anything."

**The Hebrew Bible** clearly shows that it was God's original will that we should be vegetarian (see Genesis 1:29–30). It also prophesies a time when there will be universal peace and harmony among all creatures (see Isaiah 11:1–9).

**St. Francis of Assisi stated so beautifully,** "Not to hurt our humble brethren is our first duty to them, but to stop there is not enough. We have a higher mission—to be of service to them wherever they require it."

**His Holiness Pope John Paul II said,** "Animals possess a soul and men must love and feel solidarity with our smaller brethren... the fruit of the creative action of the Holy Spirit and merit respect... as near to God as men are... He also reminded people that all living beings came into being because of the "breath" of God. He spoke of St. Francis' love for animals declaring, "We, too, are called to a similar attitude."

**Mother Teresa stated**, "They (animals) too, are created by the same loving hand of God which Created us...It is our duty to protect them and to promote their well-being."

**Mahatma Gandhi wrote**, "I do not regard flesh food as necessary for us. I hold flesh food to be unsuited to our species."

**From the Mahabharata** (one of the two major Sanskrit epics of ancient India): "We bow to all beings with great reverence in the thought and knowledge that God enters into them through fractioning Himself as living creatures."

**From the Qur'ān** (the central religious text of Islam): "There is not an animal on the earth, nor a flying creature on two wings, but they are people like unto you."

**Zen Master Thich Thanh Tu said**, "Being a vegetarian makes it easier for us to increase our loving kindness and compassion." (from *Udumbara Flowers, Book II*, Buddhism)

**Buddha** will be discussed in further detail in our Wisdom from the Past chapter. However, his belief in compassion towards all living beings was evident when he said,

"When a man has pity on all living creatures then only is he noble."

Regarding Buddhism, Albert Einstein said, "The religion of the future will be a cosmic religion. It should transcend a personal God and avoid dogmas and theology. Covering both the natural and the spiritual, it should be based on a religious sense arising from the experience of all things, natural and spiritual as a meaningful unity. If there is any religion that would cope with modern scientific needs, it would be Buddhism."

**Hinduism's** teachings include the transmigration of souls (samsara). It is one of the many religions that have extended the logical implications of its principles to include all creatures. Many wonderful statements have been made to testify to the Hindu belief in doing no harm, including, "Meat cannot be obtained without injury to animals, and the slaughter of animals obstructs the way to Heaven; let him therefore shun the use of meat," and "It is therefore the duty of all scripturally and morally conscientious Hindus to embrace a strictly vegetarian diet, avoiding all forms of meat, fish, and eggs."

**From The Laws of Manu V, 45–52** (*The Manu Smriti* or *Laws of Manu* is one of the most important and earliest Hindu texts): "He who does not willingly cause the pain of confinement and death to living beings, but desires the good of all, obtains endless bliss. He who injures no creature obtains without effort what he thinks of, what he strives for, and what he fixes his mind on. Flesh meats cannot be procured without injury to animals, and the slaughter of animals is not conducive to heavenly bliss; from flesh meat, therefore, let man abstain."

There have been so many wonderful books written about the various religious beliefs on the treatment of animals and many insightful theologians, historians, priests, ministers, and bishops who are trying to get the message across how terribly wrong it is to cause harm to God's children, in whatever form they come. We gain a feeling of bliss and even euphoria knowing that we are doing God's work by protecting the animals.

We hope you enjoy the following stories from people who have had religion as a mainstay in their lives.

### For the Creator and the Creatures

*The Rev. Professor Andrew Linzey, Ph.D., DD, is an author, Anglican priest, theologian, writer and Christian vegetarian. He has authored or edited over twenty books on theology and ethics and written over 180 articles on the subject. For further information on Andrew Linzey, please see oxfordanimalethics.com.*

Only later did I hear my experiences described as "mystical"—"nature mysticism" in particular. At the time I thought them natural. Intense and beautiful—to be sure—but not abnormal. It came as a shock to learn that many did not apparently have these experiences and, even more so, that some people denied that they happened at all.

On reflection I now see that they were unusual. At least in the sense that they were not obviously attributable to my own social conditioning and background. My family were not, to say the least, strongly religious. My religious education was really non-existent. When at the age of fourteen I announced my desire to be ordained, my family reacted—not unnaturally—with incredulity and mirth.

The intensity of the experiences has long since passed, but I now see that they have led to two long-term consequences. The first was the desire to be a priest. That God existed, despite all my personal querulousness and doubt, was never an issue for me as it was for my contemporaries. I believed as someone convinced from early years of the existence of other worlds. There's more in heaven and earth than most people's philosophy was my experience. I have always liked the line from Malcolm Muggeridge that "a savage prostrating himself before a painted stone has always seemed to me nearer the truth than any Einstein or Bertrand Russell". I was drawn to theology because its language allowed for the discussion of the apparently incredible.

While the intensity has certainly faded, even now I recollect moments wandering around Oxford (where I lived for the first eighteen years of my life) of sublime illumination. I snatch from my memory glimpses of transfiguration. It would happen as simply as this: sitting, reflecting on the bank of a river or in a wood or in a field, my mind would focus on some natural object and gently a profound sense of well-being would well up within me. An all-pervading sense of the infinite goodness of God the Creator within all living things. An experience of being connected, made whole, one with something Other beyond yet made manifest within every particle of creation. "Andrew is getting high on nature again" was the understandable—if not entirely accurate—reproach of some of my friends.

The second consequence, though I see it now in retrospect, was a deepened empathy for the world of nature and a particular sensitivity for animals. I have always been struck by the Christ-like innocence of animals. Although I became subsequently convinced by the rational arguments against animal exploitation, they were never where my sensitivity began. Now, as ever, I am appalled and shocked by the contemporary disregard for animal life. Such feeling is sometimes too loosely dismissed as "neo-pantheism", or, even worse, "idolatry". The reverse is the case. It is the Creator who leads us into a deepened awareness of the value of all life. To feel the suffering of other creatures is divine grace.

Reading Albert Schweitzer was a revelation. His theology based on the "mysticism" of reverence for life made me realize I was not alone. "There grew in me an unshakeable conviction," he wrote, reflecting on his own childhood and adolescence, "that we have no right to inflict suffering and death on another living creature unless there is some unavoidable necessity for it, and that we ought all of us to feel what a horrible thing it is to cause suffering and death out of mere thoughtlessness...I have grown more and more certain... that we fail to acknowledge it and to carry our belief into practice chiefly because we are afraid of being laughed at by other people as sentimentalists, though partly also because we allow our best feelings to get blunted." Schweitzer vowed that he would never disguise his feelings or be afraid of the "reproach of sentimentalism".

I too have made a similar vow. And in the process I have found the many-sidedness of theology—despite the increasing fundamentalism of so many churches—both an illumination and a grace. For at the centre of Christian theology is the Word made flesh, God sentient and crucified. A way of divine power so powerful that it is made real in powerlessness, humility, gentleness and self-costly loving. Sensitivity to God's creation follows inexorably from faith in God the Creator—or should do. I do not know what it means to be a Christian and not to lay before oneself the goal of becoming a more sensitive, gentle, loving, forgiving person.

Our cruel, harsh and exploitative attitude to nature, and animals in particular, stems from spiritual blindness. We do not see that the lives of other living creatures have value and worth beyond our narrow anthropocentric horizons. The truth is that our concept of God is still dreadfully narrow. We have failed to connect, to perceive the significances of other worlds, and to feel their pain. We have lost what D. H. Lawrence once called "the sixth sense of wonder".

What I cannot deny is that the Spirit was present in my early experiences in a way that I now see that the Spirit is operative within the whole realm of creation itself. The Spirit which animates all life is also the source of all goodness, beauty and creativity not least in poetry, literature, art, music and thinking. What I once thought was a personal, localized set of experiences in my home town is what I have now come to see as the experience open and real to all in every truly creative human experience. "Whatever we create, however truly it reflects our creation, is always invested with something more powerful than the selves which have produced it," wrote Laurens van der Post. "The power and the glory is at our service, but never of our invention."

*Andrew's story is a revised version of his contribution to Dan Cohn-Sherbok (ed.),* Glimpses of God. *Duckworth, 1994.* © *Andrew Linzey*

## Veganism as Service to God

*Carol Meyer, a former nun with an M.A. in Theology, and now a spiritual teacher, grew up, like so many of us, eating animals. But as she traveled her spiritual path, she was determined to make her values consistent in every avenue of her life. This led to an irrevocable, heartfelt decision and a "spiritual gift of immense proportions".*

Growing up on a Kansas farm, I ate meat almost three times a day. Fortunately, we raised the animals, so they were treated humanely and weren't loaded with the toxins, hormones and antibiotics found in most meat today. In my 30s, I visited my first health food store, learned red meat wasn't good for me, so stopped eating it almost immediately. Over the years as I learned more, I gradually moved to becoming a vegan. I find this choice inseparably entwined with my spiritual life and values. All I know is that a plant-based diet is an intrinsic part of who I am. It's not an option. It's not negotiable. I am firmly and irrevocably committed to this path for life because I know in my heart it is the right one.

I can't really explain how I got here. I've always been a Catholic and have taken my relationship to God seriously. Because I've sincerely sought to love and serve God, God has led me into arenas of social justice, environmental concern, peace activism and non-violence. My regular meditation practice has heightened my consciousness and sense of oneness and compassion for all things. As my awareness and knowledge about the negative effects of raising animals for food has grown, it's solidified my inner convictions about being a vegan.

Walking on this non-mainstream path without a lot of outside support has caused me to be spiritually stronger. It's taught me to trust my inner guidance and the voice of God even when friends and the culture try to persuade me otherwise. I've learned to accept myself as "different" than most people, content to be in a small company of comrades, rather than seeking safety and belonging in conforming to the eating patterns of the masses.

Being a vegan has challenged me to be non-judgmental of those who do eat meat and animal products. I remind myself that people are on their own path with God and can only act out of their current level of awareness and spiritual development. I find it takes a lot of discernment to know when to speak up about this issue and when to just quietly witness to my values. I feel a call to educate and raise consciousness, but I don't want my zeal to overshadow kindness and humility.

As a Christian, I believe my body is a temple of the Holy Spirit, not my personal possession to use and abuse. I consider my vegan diet the best way to keep this temple healthy, so I can do God's work in the world and it can be a servant to my spiritual growth. I know that our bodies are not designed to eat meat and that doing so weakens and harms them. I believe all the suffering, fear and violence inflicted on factory-farmed animals come to rest in the tissues of the people who eat these animals and their milk, eggs, and cheese. I seek to have only positive energy feed my body and soul. Indeed, I feel lighter, clearer and more harmonious than I did when I ate meat years ago.

The Gospel values of concern for the poor and oppressed have always resonated with me. I am thrilled that my sphere of concern has expanded to include all living things. I keep before me the image of ten billion pairs of animal eyes looking at me, silently pleading for help in their suffering. I constantly send them love and pray for their release, even as I do my small part to change the systems that oppress my animal kin.

Being a vegan is no burden at all. It is a spiritual gift of immense proportions. I am deeply grateful to God for all the people who have gone before me on this path, enabling me to partake of its riches and perhaps carry the movement forward. I feel so blessed to be in a growing, mutually loving relationship with all creation and its creatures, rather than exploiting them for my own ends. I envision a world in which all people, animals and creation live in a mutually-enhancing way, in blessed union with the divine Creator of love.

*Carol, founder of WisdomWays Spirituality Ministries,
teaches holistic spirituality classes, offers Spiritual Direction,
and does therapeutic massage. Her class topics include meditation,
veganism, holistic health, simple living, earth stewardship, and living
in the moment. Her quarterly spirituality newsletter,*
WisdomWays, *is available at www.wisdom-ways.org.*

## Why I Am Vegan

*Richard H. Schwartz, Ph.D., Professor Emeritus, College of Staten Island, is author of* Judaism and Vegetarianism, Judaism and Global Survival, *and* Mathematics and Global Survival, *and over 130 articles. He is President of Jewish Vegetarians of North America (JVNA), co-founder of the Society of Ethical and Religious Vegetarians (SERV), and associate producer of the film* A Sacred Duty *(asacredduty.com).*

Until 1978, I was a "meat and potatoes" man. My mother would be sure to prepare my favorite dish, pot roast, whenever I came to visit with my wife and children. It was a family tradition that I would be served a turkey drumstick every Thanksgiving. Yet, I not only became a vegan, but I now devote a major part of my time to writing, speaking, and teaching about the benefits of veganism. What caused this drastic change?

In 1973 I began teaching a course, "Mathematics and the Environment" at the College of Staten Island. The course uses basic mathematical concepts and problems to explore current critical issues, such as pollution, resource scarcities, hunger, energy, population growth, the arms race, nutrition, and health. While reviewing material related to world hunger, I became aware of the tremendous waste of grain associated with the production of beef at a time when millions of the world's people were malnourished. In spite of my own eating habits, I often led class discussions on the possibility of reducing meat consumption as a way of helping hungry people. After several semesters of this, I took my own advice and gave up eating red meat, while continuing to eat chicken and fish.

I then began to read about the many health benefits of vegetarianism and about the horrible conditions for animals raised on factory farms. I was increasingly attracted to vegetarianism, and on January 1, 1978, I decided to join the International Jewish Vegetarian Society. I had two choices for membership: (1) practicing vegetarian (one who refrains from eating any flesh); (2) non-vegetarian (one who is in sympathy with the movement, while not yet a vegetarian). I decided to become a full practicing vegetarian, and since then have avoided eating any meat, fowl, or fish.

Since that decision, besides learning much about vegetarianism's connections to health, nutrition, ecology, resource usage, hunger, and the treatment of animals, I also started investigating connections between vegetarianism and Judaism. I learned that the first biblical dietary law (Genesis 1:29) is to be strictly vegetarian, and I became convinced that important Jewish mandates to preserve our health, be kind to animals, protect the environment, conserve natural resources, share with hungry people, and seek and pursue peace all point to vegetarianism as the best diet for Jews (and everyone else). To get this message to a wider audience I wrote a book, *Judaism and Vegetarianism*, which was first published in 1982. (Revised, expanded editions were published in 1988 and 2001.)

I gradually moved toward veganism and became a practicing vegan around 2000. Increasingly, as I learned about the realities of animal-based diets and their inconsistency with Jewish values, I have come to see veganism as not only an important personal choice, but also a societal imperative, an essential component to the solution of many national and global problems.

I have been spending much time trying to make others aware of the importance of switching toward vegetarianism or, preferably, veganism, both for themselves and for the world. I have appeared on over 100 radio and cable television programs; had many letters and several op-ed articles in a variety of publications; spoken frequently at the College of Staten Island and to community groups; given over 30 talks and met with three chief rabbis and other religious and political leaders in Israel, while visiting my two daughters and their families. In 1987, I was selected as "Jewish Vegetarian of the Year" by the Jewish Vegetarians of North America and in 2005 I was inducted into the North American Vegetarian Society's "Hall of Fame".

I have always felt good about my decision to become a vegetarian and more recently a vegan. Putting principles and values into practice is far more valuable and rewarding than hours of preaching. I feel strongly that my spirituality, sensitivity and compassion have been enhanced by my dietary shifts and my efforts to share information with others. When people ask me why I gave up meat and other animal products, I welcome the opportunity to explain the many benefits of veganism.

Recently, I have noted signs of increased interest in vegetarianism, and a growing number of people are concerned about dietary connections to health, nutrition, animal rights, and ecology. Yet, consumption of animal products seems to be increasing even as evidence increases that this is contributing to an epidemic of diseases and to global warming and other environmental threats that are moving the world rapidly toward a potential unprecedented catastrophe. So there is much that still needs to be done. My hope is to be able to keep learning, writing, and speaking about veganism, to help bring closer that day when, in the words of the motto of the International Jewish Vegetarian Society, "No one shall hurt nor destroy in all of God's holy mountain." (Isaiah 11:9)

*Learn more about Richard at JewishVeg.com.*

# CHAPTER ELEVEN

# Sanctuary Saviors

*Think occasionally of the suffering
of which you spare yourself the sight.*
Albert Schweitzer

Sanctuary founders—what endearing people. The unbearable tragedy and suffering they witness during the rescues they perform must be utterly heart wrenching.

I, Tina, was lucky enough to be a small part of the work of rescuing three lambs. Initially Animal Acres rescued them and many other animals after they were abandoned at a foreclosed property. They had been without food or water for an undetermined amount of time. Frank, the manager of Animal Acres, kindly drove them to my ranch in Arizona last spring. One of them, Bitsy, lost her mother before she could receive the important nutrients from her milk and had to be bottle fed when she first arrived at my home.

I must say that the love and companionship I share with these lambs is enormous. I believe that because they endured such hardship, they are more appreciative of human love and care. Whatever the case, these three little critters, Andy, Joey and Bitsy, have enhanced my life in a way I never believed possible. When times get rough and I need a little love, peace and solitude, this is where I turn. To see them running toward me when I get close to their gate is so uplifting. When I do reach them, they surround me for pets and kisses, waiting patiently for their turn. They seem to crave love and attention. The time spent with them is the most spiritually cleansing time I spend in a day. There is complete and uncomplicated love and joy. These animal friends confirmed the fact that I want a farm animal sanctuary more than I've wanted anything in a very long time.

However, after speaking with some sanctuary founders, I came to learn that this work is all consuming and leaves no time for other pursuits. I have had a taste of this fact by the few animals I care for now: three lambs, eight chickens, five ducks, two turkeys, two peacocks, one red golden pheasant, two african grey parrots and two labrador retrievers. But when Hanna the chicken jumps into my lap for kisses, it melts me. This in turn leads to the desire to help more of them. Although, I'm fairly sure I could not attend a rescue and see the horrors first-hand, as the rescue teams do, or experience a rescued animal I've given my whole heart to, die from complications.

These people who video the insides of factory farms and slaughterhouses, who rescue animals who have been abandoned and those who have been affected by floods, tornadoes or hurricanes are very special people indeed. The fact that most people cannot even view a video showing cruelty to animals is some indication as to how difficult this work can be. We are blessed to have them.

## That's Some Sheep

*Lorri Houston (formerly Bauston) is considered a pioneer of the farmed animal sanctuary movement. She and Gene Baur (formerly Bauston) opened the country's first shelter for farmed animals aptly named Farm Sanctuary. Lorri has directly saved thousands of animals from the cruelties of factory farming, and has brought national attention to the plight of animals used for food production. Her work has been featured in hundreds of national and state news reports, and in several documentaries. In 2005, Lorri Houston formed the nonprofit organization Animal Acres, a Los Angeles farmed animal sanctuary and compassionate living center (AnimalAcres.org).*

In 1986, I discovered a living sheep on a stockyard "dead pile" and her rescue led me to co-found "Farm Sanctuary", the first shelter in the country for farmed animals. Hilda the sheep was my first teacher, and set me on a path to rescue thousands of other suffering farmed animals and establish the farmed animal sanctuary movement.

I was investigating the Lancaster Stockyard in Lancaster, Pennsylvania. The stockyard bought and sold thousands of animals each week, and though I didn't expect to see animals treated well, I never expected to see animals treated like "trash". I found Hilda on the stockyard "dead pile". She had been thrown on a pile of dead and decaying animals, and at first I didn't know she was alive, but she lifted her head as I approached. My partner and I rushed her to a nearby veterinarian, who determined she was suffering from heat exhaustion. One hour later, she was standing.

I was shocked to find Hilda abandoned at the stockyard, and I was appalled to learn that dumping "downed" animals (animals too sick or injured to stand) was *not* illegal in the State of Pennsylvania. We had photographs of Hilda on the deadpile. Through her identification tag we determined which trucker had dumped her, and that she had been on the dead pile for about sixteen hours before we found her. Yet local authorities would not prosecute the trucker or stockyard for cruelty to animals because abandoning sick and injured animals was considered a "normal animal agricultural practice" in Pennsylvania. Most states, including Pennsylvania, specifically exempt farmed animals from state anti-cruelty laws. Any act, no matter how cruel or inhumane, is legal.

Hilda enjoyed twelve blissful years at "Farm Sanctuary". During our years together, she showed me how much can be accomplished when people care enough to be vital participants in programs and campaigns to stop farmed animal suffering. In 1986, very few organizations were advocating for farmed animal protection, most people thought the word "vegan" was a character from *Star Trek*, and there were no shelters in the country devoted to farmed animals. Today, there are over 25 farmed animal sanctuaries throughout the country. The newest is "Animal Acres", which I opened near Los Angeles in 2005.

Animal Acres is a unique 26-acre farm, just 45 minutes from Los Angeles. With its proximity to a major metropolitan area and the entertainment capital of the world, Animal Acres is in a strong position to bring our message of compassion to millions. In our first year of operation, I saw how much an urban farmed animal sanctuary can do—and how much people wanted to have farmed animal sanctuaries in their cities. A dedicated team of over 200 people came out to help us build the sanctuary. We saved over 200 animals from slaughter, welcomed thousands of sanctuary visitors, and reached millions of people with news coverage of our efforts in the *Los Angeles Times*, the *Daily News* and other major media. Dozens of Hollywood's famous friends of farmed animals joined Animal Acres to lend their voices and support. The comedian Bill Maher stated it best when he wrote: "I'm pleased to be a supporter of Animal Acres, L.A.'s new farm animal sanctuary. This special place is giving city slickers an opportunity to get to know farm animals—and it's hard to eat a pig after you've given one a belly rub."

Within one year after we opened, we had raised the funding needed (1.2 million dollars) for the organization to purchase the property. Animal Acres is now forever owned by the cows, pigs, chickens, and other farmed animals who desperately need a home of their own—and the organization continues to grow. Although I have been involved in the farmed animal sanctuary movement since 1986, the success of Animal Acres was a reminder to me of the crucial role played by farmed animal sanctuaries—both for animal advocates and the general public.

In our own animal protection movement, farmed animal sanctuaries are helping teach animal advocates that cows, pigs, and chickens need our help, too—and the new and growing interest in farmed animal protection issues continues to prompt campaigns to ban cruel factory farming and marketing practices. Humane enforcement agencies are more willing to intervene to stop farmed animal cruelty if there is a shelter facility in the area for farmed animals. Shortly after Animal Acres opened, a California humane agency was able to conduct the first U.S. raid on a slaughterhouse for cruelty to animals, and subsequently confiscated dozens of severely neglected animals, who were then brought to Animal Acres for rehabilitation and refuge.

For people who come into contact with farmed animals only at breakfast, lunch, or dinner, farmed animal sanctuaries provide a positive way for the public to learn that farmed animals are friends, not food. Sanctuary visitors interact with the "animal ambassadors" while being educated on the harsh truth of how farmed animals are treated to produce meat, milk, and eggs. It's just a little easier for people to hear about the cruelties of dairy production when they are getting a big cow lick. Even the youngest sanctuary visitor "gets it" after giving a pig a belly rub and sampling a veggie hotdog. Farmed animal sanctuaries make it fun—and profound.

As a founder of Farm Sanctuary, and now Animal Acres, I have personally seen thousands of people "touched" by a farmed animal, and then make the decision to save ALL farmed animals by going vegetarian or vegan. Those of us involved in direct rescue efforts for farmed animals recognize the only way to "be the change" is to use the sanctuary to open peoples' hearts and minds to the plight of farmed animals.

Every year, over ten billion animals are raised, transported, and slaughtered under the most inhumane and cruel conditions possible. During my own investigations of the meat, dairy, and egg industries, I have witnessed more suffering than I could have imagined in my worst nightmare. At hatcheries, I have seen tiny day-old chicks thrown alive into trash dumpsters because they were male and could not be used for egg production. I have given water to thirsty "downed" cows who were left suffering for hours, in parking lots, with temperatures over 100 degrees. I have looked into the hopeless eyes of calves chained to veal crates, unable to walk or even turn around. I've watched in horror as pigs with broken legs dragged themselves to the killing floor, as they were kicked and shocked by slaughterhouse workers.

People often ask me what is the hardest part of doing farmed animal rescue and sanctuary work. Witnessing animal cruelty is very difficult, but leaving suffering animals behind is devastating. Over the years, I have had to make hundreds of "Sophie's Choices" —choosing which ones to save, and which ones to leave behind. I remember the hardest rescue I ever worked on like it happened only yesterday—the Buckeye Egg Farm Rescue.

The Buckeye Egg Farm in Ohio is a typical egg production factory farm. To produce eggs, four to five hens are crammed into a bare wire cage about the size of a folded newspaper. The confinement is so severe, the hens cannot walk, stretch their wings, or even lie down comfortably. The Buckeye Egg Farm was one of the largest egg production facilities in the country, housing 14 million hens in large warehouses which held 80–100,000 birds per building. Tornadoes struck the Buckeye Egg Farm facility, and overnight, over one million birds became trapped in demolished buildings.

There was no way to prepare myself for the devastation, and the suffering. The warehouses which housed the birds had been severely damaged, and most of the buildings were missing sides, roofs, or both. Most of the birds were still trapped in the mangled cages without access to food or water. For several days, we tried to rescue as many hens as we could, while urging the owners of the facility to remove hens from cages as quickly as possible and humanely euthanize the ones that could not be taken to sanctuaries. On my last trip to the Buckeye Egg Farm, the birds had been in the cages without food or water for twelve days. I expected to see birds weak and near death—what I saw instead were birds who were very much alive and moving frantically in their cages.

The Buckeye Egg Farm would not allow animal groups to help release birds from cages, claiming it was "too dangerous" to allow non-employees to enter demolished areas. They agreed to let us have as many hens as we could take, but we had to agree to this stipulation. Still, there were times I had to make a mad dash to a cage of hens. I approached one cage that was smashed in half and reached down to pick up a bird who was caught in the wire of a mangled cage. I tucked the hen safely into my shirt, and then I tried to pry open the cage bars to rescue another hen who had her wing caught in the wire—but I was forced to leave the area before I could get her. The look on her face will never leave me. I also had to break the rules when I saw birds stuck in the manure slurry pits that accumulated under the cages. The live birds were slowly sinking into the wet manure. I got three birds out of the pit before I was stopped.

After a great deal of pressure, the Buckeye Egg Farm agreed to remove trapped birds and euthanize them. The "bird removal" crew consisted of six to eight workers to remove almost 100,000 birds from piles of debris and mangled cages. It was agonizingly slow, and cruel. The workers grabbed the birds by the legs and threw them into a tractor loading bucket. The tractor then drove to a large trailer, and dumped the live birds into it. The birds fell, flapping their wings and screaming, onto the other birds in the trailer, who lay dead, or dying. A tarp was then pulled over the trailer, and carbon dioxide gas was pumped into it for five minutes. When the tarp was pulled back, many of the birds lay gasping until the next loader full of birds was dumped on top of them.

After attempting to remove and euthanize birds for a few days, Buckeye Egg Farm halted its bird removal effort, and sent in bulldozers. Hundreds of thousands of birds were crushed and buried alive.

We documented all of this cruelty and death. The endless rows of trapped birds. The animals stuck in quick-sand-like manure pits. The birds being thrown into gas chambers and left suffocating, gasp-

ing for breath. We tried to convince authorities to prosecute the facility for animal cruelty, but we were unsuccessful. It was considered
a "natural disaster", though it was clear the suffering was caused by
the "unnatural" confinement of millions of animals. In the end, there
was nothing I could do but save as many as possible. On the last day
we were allowed in, I drove off with 500 hens. I didn't glance back as
we pulled away...I couldn't.

It is hard to witness animal cruelty and leave suffering animals
behind—and when I am struggling to cope with my anger and grief,
I try to remember another animal teacher who crossed my path, a
hen named Henny.

When I was directing Farm Sanctuary's shelters, I received a call
from the ASPCA that a chicken needed a home—a chicken that
had somehow managed to escape from a factory farm, and ended
up on a New York City bus. Fortunately, the kind driver knew this
was a chicken in trouble, and drove her to the ASPCA. At the time,
our New York shelter was completely full because of the Buckeye
Egg Farm rescue. We didn't have any rehabilitation pens open at
our shelter, but after hearing about her heroic escape, I just couldn't
say no. So, until she was healthy enough to be with the other shelter
chickens, Henny moved in with us.

At the time, my family consisted of four dogs, three cats, two
humans (and now one chicken), and we were all residing in a small,
one bedroom cabin. I didn't want Henny to be locked alone into
the bathroom, so I cautiously let her into the main room, keeping a
particularly watchful eye on the dogs. I was concerned that Henny
would be intimidated and not "fit in", but I didn't have to worry for
long—at least about the chicken. The dogs were the first to learn
that Henny would rule the roost. The minute my largest dog KJ
stuck her nose into her, Henny gave KJ a peck on the nose—clearly
there was going to be no dog "nosing" in this household. This chick-
en had attitude—she was from New York City alright. Later that
night, after everyone seemed to settle in and things were starting
to get peaceful, I was relaxing on the couch with Pierre (cat) in my
lap. Henny walked over to the couch, surveyed the situation, and

then jumped on to my lap—which of course meant, she also jumped on to the cat. Pierre leaped into the air hissing and screaming and Henny didn't ruffle a feather. She just calmly settled into my lap, ignoring the glaring cat, and started cooing.

The first night, I put her into a bedded carrier so she (and the rest of us) could sleep soundly throughout the night. She didn't seem to like this idea, and I felt a little guilty as her eyes followed me into the bedroom. That night, she must have worked her way into my dreams, because I woke up knowing I couldn't put her in the carrier again. By now, everyone had accepted Henny into the household, so it seemed safe enough to just let her find her own sleeping spot in the house. The big dogs grabbed the couch, the cats and small dogs jumped on our bed, and we all crawled under the covers. Within seconds, I heard the tiny "click-click-click" of Henny's feet, and they were coming closer and closer. I peered over the side of the bed, and there was Henny, looking up. I'd seen this look before—Henny was going to jump on to the bed. I went to the bathroom and grabbed a towel for the bed, and Henny jumped up and slept with us until dawn. (In case you're wondering, Henny was "housebroken" and never had an "incident" on the bed or furniture.)

At night when Henny and I cuddled together, I was amazed by her trusting and loving nature. She was, after all, a hen who had lived her entire life under cruel factory farm conditions. She had suffered "debeaking" a painful mutilation that involves cutting off the tip of hens' beaks to reduce pecking injuries because the birds are so severely overcrowded. Then, for months, she had endured intensive confinement in a bare wire cage with several other hens—a cage so small that she could not even stretch her wings. Finally, when she was no longer "productive" she was literally torn from her cage and thrown into a transportation truck headed for slaughter. Bruised, battered and worn-out laying hens are ground up and used for pot pies and baby food.

In the few weeks she stayed with us, I discovered that Henny was curious and intelligent (she learned in one night to stay on the towel in her corner of the bed). Henny was fearless and self-assured

(I learned this when I saw her "take on" a ninety pound growling dog because SHE wanted the chew toy). Henny was friendly (she greeted me at the door each day after work and then followed me around like a puppy dog). And, Henny loved to be loved (and gave me enormous amounts of love in return).

Henny had never known a kind touch from a human. Humans had only inflicted fear, pain and endless days of torment. Yet, she had chosen to bring us into HER family—a family filled with generosity, forgiveness, and hope. It was a sad day when Henny was ready to be with her own people (well, maybe not so sad for my companion dogs and cats), but I was grateful for the time I had with this remarkable teacher, who reminded me of all that one chicken, or person, can be.

My biggest mission in life is to teach people that farmed animals ARE animals. Animals who feel pain or comfort, or joy or sorrow, just like a dog or cat. Farmed animal sanctuaries provide the opportunity for people to learn, and love. Colin, a newborn goat brought to Animal Acres, taught us to love, even when our hearts are breaking.

Colin was taken from his mother when he was just a day or two old. Like male calves, male goats are taken to livestock auctions as soon as they are born and sold for meat production. We don't know who bought Colin, but we do know little Colin was purchased by humans whose hearts had turned to stone.

Colin was abandoned in a canyon late at night—with both of his ears cut off. One ear had been completely severed and the other ear had been cut off half way. His cries were heard by two responsible individuals who intervened to help, and took Colin to local authorities. Within 24 hours, Colin had found safe refuge at Animal Acres. After determining he needed immediate medical attention, our veterinarian performed corrective surgery and repaired both ears. Because of his condition, Colin couldn't be with the other goats and sheep yet, so he lived in the sanctuary ranch house or offices at night, and the visitor courtyard during the day.

Despite all he had been through, Colin was one of most loving and friendly animals we have ever met. He always wanted to be near people, and liked to sit in visitors' laps. At night, he would sleep on the couch or his fluffy "blankie" on the floor. Our little "house-goat" became a beloved member of our sanctuary family, and he deeply touched everyone who met him.

Sadly, surgery, veterinary care, and hours of love weren't enough to save Colin. Since he lacked essential nutrients from his mom's milk, his immune system was too weak. Colin passed away peacefully in his sleep one night on his favorite blankie. We were devastated. Our grief turned into anger as we gathered to bury him. His grave was filled with roses from the sanctuary courtyard, and locks from our hair (he loved to chew on peoples' hair). Then, one by one, we started remembering how Colin had done so much in his short time on earth to teach people to extend compassion to farmed animals too. It was as if our littlest angel was watching, and reminding us never to let hate or anger consume our compassion and love.

We remembered that Colin loved humans, even after humans had tortured him.

We remembered how Colin would smile whenever people were petting him.

We remembered how Colin wanted to be a part of our Country Hoedown and stood for hours to be kissed and cuddled.

We remembered his last day on earth, when he taught over 60 visiting school children to be kind to ALL animals.

And we remembered how he motivated people to protect farmed animals. Everyone who met Colin wanted to help. When we asked the school children what they should do if they see someone hurt an animal like Colin, the kids replied: "Tell someone who can help," "Call the police," and "Take the animal to a safe place like here (Animal Acres)."

One Animal Acres member posted Colin's picture and story on an animal message forum, and the responses brought more tears to our eyes. One person wrote: "It is always uplifting to me that with everything an animal can go through, they can still respond so readily to love and care." Another wrote: "I'm so sorry his life was so short, but at the very end, the horrors he had gone through were replaced with love overflowing beyond measure. I hope those school children will take that lesson with them for the rest of their lives and use it to do good for animals."

Colin knew that hate and anger don't change the world—and he reminded us that we must always turn anger into compassion, and compassion into action.

For the first time in history, people are seeing cows, pigs, and chickens as living, feeling animals, and it is changing the way society views and treats farmed animals. When people learn about the suffering farmed animals endure, they are shocked and appalled, and they go vegetarian, and/or vote to stop abusive farming practices. In addition to the creation of dozens of new farmed animal sanctuaries, the past ten years have ushered in laws and initiatives banning cruel animal agriculture practices, along with the introduction of vegetarian and vegan food options at almost every major supermarket and restaurant throughout the country. Through farmed animal sanctuaries, farmed animals themselves finally have a voice. They are their own advocates—and perhaps that is why the farmed animal sanctuary movement is so successful.

At times, working on behalf of ten billion suffering animals is heartbreaking, and daunting. But Hilda, Henny, Colin, and the other farmed animals have touched my life, and have given me hope —because each and every person CAN do something to stop the suffering NOW, simply by choosing what, or whom, to eat.

## Heart of Stone to a Heart of Love

*Michael E. Sowders' life-changing story (as told by Olivia Rue) reminds us once again of the profound effect the tiniest animal visitors can have on the human heart. Michael explains in such a moving and beautiful way how a broken heart can be the very doorway through which one finds inner peace and compassion. Following his transformation, Michael founded the Lifetime Friends Animal Sanctuary (ltfas.org).*

I went from having a heart of stone to a heart of love. From a cold, emotionless state to one of warmth and compassion. Because of the vivid change that God has made in my life, I am compelled to share my story. I hope it may inspire others to open their hearts.

Growing up under a constant barrage of verbal, sexual and emotional abuse had left me feeling empty inside. At some point, my despair had led me to make a choice to not feel anything for anyone. As a young man, I moved to the mountains of north Idaho, hoping to find or create my true self.

One day at my cabin "in the middle of nowhere", a little tabby cat showed up on my doorstep. Having no interest in animals, I shoved him away. For three months he persisted, visiting frequently, undaunted by my lack of welcome. Finally, I gave in and fed him. A month later, I invited the little cat into the house, named him Jake, and an amazing relationship was born. Within a few days, Jake was curling up on my bed at night, his soft fur and contented purr bringing a comforting presence I hadn't known I needed. Over the next two years, he became my closest friend, a wonderful companion who accepted me as I was and loved me unconditionally. When he died from crushing snow that fell from the rooftop, it was the first time in years that I had felt real pain.

My anguish was too much to take—I couldn't handle such strong feelings of loss. So I medicated the pain, over-using prescription drugs to dull my senses and avoid having to feel.

A year passed before I had the strength to visit the shelter and adopt two cats: Buffie and Woofers. Buffie died of liver failure two years later. Though I knew I had done everything I could to help him, still I grieved over his loss for over a year.

But something remarkable was happening to me. As I felt love and sadness for these animals, I sensed another presence in my softened heart: God's love. I realized in amazement that He was using the grief process to help strip me of layers of emotional callousness, indifference and detachment. I had worked so hard over the years to build this tough, protective shell, yet with each beat of my aching heart there was another crack, and another layer slipped away, exposing me—revealing my true self. And healing the pain. God was healing me, and using the giftings of animals to get to my stony heart. Through God and His messengers Jake, Buffie and Woofers, I was learning the values of mutual respect, companionship, acceptance, courtesy, tolerance, validation and true friendship. A level of wholeness was filling my soul and enhancing my life.

During this time, I also learned about the torture that farm animals go through before they are killed and actually felt broken and grief-stricken for their suffering. Because of them, I made the choice to become vegan. There is nothing humane about eating animals or their eggs or milk, and there is nothing humane about using the skins of animals who are treated with indifference and callousness and sometimes skinned alive.

Feeling called to help the creatures that God had brought into my life, I sold my mountain home and relocated to land better suited to my plans…I knew what to do: I founded Lifetime Friends Animal Sanctuary (LTFAS).

At the Sanctuary, I have finally made the choice to stop burying my feelings. When, despite all of our efforts to save him or her, a rescuee dies, I no longer run from the pain. I feel the hurt, I cry the tears, I mourn the loss. And I pray. I pray that God's angels will gently carry that precious soul home to Him.

And there have been so many other wonderful, life-affirming changes in me! God has freed me from several afflictions which I had developed as a consequence of childhood abuse, including addictions to TV, videos, alcohol, prescription drugs and emotional turmoil. One of my favorite Bible passages is John 8:36: "Whom the Son sets free is free indeed, from the inside out."

So, just opening my heart, my soul and my life to these hurting creatures of God has enriched my life immeasurably. Founding and continuing LTFAS has unleashed the power of compassion in me, and healing benefits are far-reaching. I've learned that manhood is not about being feeling-less, but being of strong mind and tender heart. I've chosen mercy and compassion and a gentle way of being. I now have the ability to communicate and connect with a being outside of myself. I cherish the sweet bonds that develop with each new animal companion that comes into my life. I, and this organization, have the purpose and passion to responsibly provide a home for stray, abandoned and abused animals.

I believe that being in the right relationship with God allows me to be emotionally capable of enjoying healthy relationships with myself and others. The quote I wrote to place on LTFAS literature sums up this belief: "Love for an animal companion becomes something transforming that gave this man back feelings that were lost or buried, thus unexpectedly, immeasurably enriching his life."

## A Special Day at Catskill

*Kathy Stevens is founder and director of Catskill Animal Sanctuary (casanctuary.org) and author of* Where the Blind Horse Sings: Love and Healing at an Animal Sanctuary. *In her story she shares an extraordinary visit with her animal friends.*

Catskill Animal Sanctuary in upstate New York, home on any given day to 200 rescued farm animals, is a breathlessly bustling place. In fact, I've never once walked into our main barn during work hours and not seen a human. Not once in the eight years since we opened. But today it happened. Alex was up in the large hill pasture reinforcing fences because two mules were due to arrive Sunday as their family's farm was in foreclosure. One of them, Blackjack, is nicknamed Houdini—"Got a weak section, he'll find it," his owner had explained.

Meanwhile, staffers Lorraine, Betsy, and volunteers Mary Ellen and China were cleaning the large cow barn at the back of the farm. Only I didn't know this.

My dog Murphy, Director of Canine Pursuits, and I walked into the barn. "Where's Lorraine?" I asked the yellow mutt, who trotted toward the kitchen halfway down the aisle in search of his pal. Murphy takes his job seriously.

Five feet from the kitchen entrance, Rambo the sheep lay in the middle of the aisle, holding court. Beside him stood Norma Jean the turkey, gently pulling bits of hay from Rambo's wool. Potbellies Zoey, Charlie, and Ozzie were there too; surprisingly, they weren't searching for food. They were simply there, enjoying the company of their friends.

I plopped down with them. Murphy did too, right by my side. To my delight, the animals allowed us to enter their peaceful circle—and just *to be* with them. No one charged over to beg for food; neither did anyone walk away because a dog and a human had entered their space. Hannah, Rambo's woolly pal, the sheep found in a Queens cemetery by Anne Marie Lucas of *Animal Cops* fame, strolled over to nuzzle Murphy the way she always does. Mufasa the goat was with her. Above all of us, Max, a sweet old quarter horse approaching forty, hung his big head over the four-foot stall wall, and there we were together: two sheep, a turkey, a goat, three pigs, a horse, a dog, and a human.

For a few precious, peaceful minutes we sat…that's all. Miraculous simplicity.

But then Claude, the giant pink pig with the bad leg that earned him free-range status lest he be picked on by the stronger, more dominant pigs in the pig pasture…Claude strolled in from the far end of the barn.

"Hey, big man…hey sweet pig," I called softly to him. A few heads turned in his direction.

"Mmmph…" he responded. And then he walked not into his stall the way he typically would, but past it, straight toward us. He walked right up to Max the horse, his scratchy pink back nearly level with Max's muzzle, and he lifted his snout to Max and there they were, wet pink pig nose pressing into soft black horse nose. They stood there, pig to horse, Claude looking up intently, somehow knowing that Max would not lunge at him the way the horses typically do at the big pigs.

Laugh, shake your head, call me anthropomorphic if you're skeptical or obtuse or disconnected, but I experienced what I experienced, and what I experienced on a cold November day was pigs and turkeys and goats and humans and horses and sheep and dogs enjoying each other's company. Happy just to be.

Why humans continue to inflict the horrors we do upon the animal kingdom is difficult for folks like me to accept. At Catskill Animal Sanctuary, we do all that we can to encourage thousands of annual guests to see "food animals" as I have seen them in this very special moment. They are my friends; they are my teachers. They are not my food.

# CHAPTER TWELVE

## Judy and Tina's Stories

*As we talked of freedom and justice one day for all,*
*we sat down to steaks. I am eating misery, I thought,*
*as I took the first bite. And spit it out.*
Alice Walker

We thought you might like to hear our stories too—how it was that we came to commit ourselves to this ahimsa life and how we found our way to joy and hope for the future of the planet, the animals, and one another.

## God's Lambs by Judy

I, like most young children, was shielded from the violence of the world initially. The majority of children's storybooks bear witness to that. It is almost as if the adults who write them are saying, "No, really, earth is a paradise where animals and people live together in harmony, and horses and cows and pigs come into the house with the dogs, and everybody is happy." I have yet to find a children's book that ends with pictures of the beloved animals lying slaughtered and bleeding.

Yet, eventually this fantasy crumbles, and the truth about what human beings really do to animals (not to mention other people and nature) can no longer be kept from the children. Though we may not remember it, the loss of that belief in a paradise affects us with a deep and penetrating grief about which few of us speak.

It is at such a point in our young lives that we feel the need to ease this vague and untitled pain and find inner peace. It is a longing to reconnect with animals and nature and feel again that precious kinship. It is a longing to find the paradise we thought existed here, and for some, it becomes a lifelong goal to create that kind and peaceful world, regardless of the odds against it.

The beginning of the disconnection is well illustrated in this example. A four year old I know whose father hunts birds, once explained to me that the birds are "bad". When I asked him why, he said, "Well, Daddy hates them, so he kills them." In order to make sense of the fact that his gentle, adoring dad would do such harm, he decided on his own, that the birds must be really bad.

Looking back on my life, I think my lost paradise came into sharp focus with the lambs. I was ten years old when every kid's dream came true for me. My family moved to the edge of town onto seven acres with a pasture. A pasture! That meant we could share our lives with more animals, and that sounded just perfect to me.

When the sheep arrived to live with us and have their babies, I fell in love with them, of course. In my naïve imagination, we would always be together. I spent as much time as I could with them. They were so perfectly innocent, and they loved to be hugged and cuddled. Each one had his or her own special personality. Holding them was like holding a little piece of heaven. I loved to look at the picture of Jesus holding a lamb in his arms, and it gave me a sense of the sacredness of these precious beings and their mystical connection to divine love.

Then one day, as you have already no doubt guessed, I came home from school to an empty pasture. No lambs. No warning. No chance to save them. Where had they been taken? Yet my tears at their loss were nothing in comparison to the next shock I was to experience.

It was dinnertime, and the table was filled with the usual meal over which my mother had faithfully labored. The big hunk of meat was, as usual, the centerpiece of the meal and, somehow, a symbol that we were prospering and well-fed. And then it happened. Someone —I don't recall who, but someone who knew, spoke glowingly of the delicious lamb we were eating.

There it was, for me, as for so many of us, the sudden, overwhelming realization that meat comes from the animals we love, animals we see in books, animals in pastures, animals whom we know personally; animals whose eyes once shone brightly with the joy of living. I might as well have discovered I was eating my dog. I was inconsolable. What kind of world was I living in where friends ate friends; where innocent, defenseless animals were taught to trust and then be taken away without goodbyes, brutally killed and devoured?

Such things are called the loss of innocence in children. It is also the loss of innocents, the terrible loss of billions of innocent beings. And historically, both losses have taken an immense toll on the soul of humanity.

From that point on, I did not want to eat meat. (It took me many more years to learn about the suffering inherent in milk and eggs.) However, this was the '50s in Kansas. My father was a hunter. My uncles ran the stockyards and slaughterhouse. I had never heard of vegetarians; perhaps my parents hadn't either. I became known as "woolly minded" for not wanting to eat animals. I guess I was, since it was the woolly lambs themselves who transformed and renewed my mind. So I ate very little meat and fed a lot to the dogs under the table.

It was confusing. There was so much pride about such a brutal thing. We occasionally would eat at the Golden Ox, a restaurant built on the edge of the stockyards. The Kansas City steaks were famous, I was told. The stench of dead and dying cows outside the restaurant was horrific, but inside everyone seemed happy. As I flashed back to the storybooks in which kids and cows were friends, it all blurred together for me in a confusing mess. As kids, we can't articulate it, but what we are feeling is, "This isn't the way the world is supposed to be. What is going on?"

Meanwhile, to add to the confusion, my father—bless his heart—was a big game hunter. Our home décor included a dead polar bear made into a rug (shot by him in Alaska), a dead zebra made into a rug (shot by him in Africa), and numerous animals' heads looking down at me from the walls. Dad didn't hate these animals. He simply thought he had the right to kill them (including entire families for museum displays).

Dad killed hundreds of animals, including wolves from a plane, many mammals and beautiful birds, and uncounted fish. Favorite guests in our home included many a hunter and fisherman who loved to share their stories over glasses of bourbon and scotch. The air of respect and admiration that filled the house for Dad and these folks was palpable. Indeed, many, like my father, were medical doctors and other professionals who made great contributions to the human community.

For this and other reasons, I remained puzzled and wondered if something was wrong with me, because the juxtaposition of admired men and ruthless killing didn't make any sense to me.

Ultimately, my search for meaning in life, to find an explanation for all the violence and to find my own way continued onward. Somehow, my quest to do what I could to stop the suffering of others and my find my own peace became a tandem journey.

Finally, in my 20s I began hearing about vegetarianism and learning how to live in that way. As my journey has continued, we have all become more aware of the atrocities, and some reforms and some liberations have taken place. With the help of the information that came out from the many animal rights groups that formed, I began to learn that this was not just about avoiding the eating of animals. This was about changing the entire world-view of humanity toward nature and all life.

This was not just a new way to eat; this was indeed a spiritual, intellectual, ethical, and moral revolution. Realizing this, I felt compelled not only to leave off eating animals, but also to speak out for them and for the new paradigm of living in harmony with all.

In a way, it is ironic to think that one could find peace and joy when confronted with an endless litany of abuses committed by people against innocent and helpless animals, and, of course, people and nature as well. But compared to where I was as a clueless child and a young adult, I have found a peace and joy that is with me always. How can this be?

I hope that the many stories in this book show how this can happen. Perhaps it seems a stretch to say that living a vegan life can bring us peace and joy. But let us look at the broadest definition of veganism. The foundation of such a life includes doing the least harm possible in all our actions and living a life of service, nonviolence, lovingkindness, and kinship with all beings. Is it any wonder then that so many people find such precious peace by living in this way? For by giving peace, they receive exactly that in return.

As we have learned throughout this book, veganism is much more than a diet. It is a spiritual makeover of extraordinary proportions. It involves questioning absolutely everything we've been taught by our culture, de-programming our minds, finding friends who are learning to live this way, practicing being mindful and treasuring each moment instead of listening to our egos' regrets and fears.

And I have to say to you all—that sounds like a lot, but with each step, our spirits become more liberated and more joyful. And if I did it, anyone can, absolutely anyone. I certainly have not reached some pinnacle of perfection, but every day is more entrancing than the one before, and God's peace is always with me. There is just something so spirit lifting about knowing that at each meal, we are saving the lives of people and animals, and in so doing, we are demonstrating love and peace.

By doing the absolute least harm possible, we are set free to participate in the celebration of life; to look into the big eyes of a cow and know she is our friend, not our food; to feel the ecstasy of our oneness with all life; to sing praises with the crickets and frogs; to greet the fly in our house and carry her gently outside; to pray for and with the ones we cannot save; to know we are creating a better world, a new culture, with our love. That is the treasure—the missing peace found at last.

I came full circle a few months ago when I visited Farm Sanctuary in Watkins Glen, New York. There I was able to snuggle with lambs once again and bask in their sweet and peaceful presence. They were as I remembered them. Like dogs, they gathered among us asking for hugs and caresses. They looked at me so trustingly as my lamb friends had done so long ago. But the innocent trust of these lambs will not be betrayed.

May all lambs be safe from harm. May all beings be free. May all human beings awaken to universal love and ahimsa.

## My Awakening by Tina

*A human being is a part of the whole, called by us the "Universe", a part limited in time and space. He experiences himself, his thoughts and feelings, as something separate from the rest—a kind of optical delusion of his consciousness. This delusion is a kind of prison for us, restricting us to our personal desires and to affection for a few persons nearest to us. Our task must be to free ourselves from this prison by widening our circle of compassion to embrace all living creatures and the whole of nature in its beauty. Nobody is able to achieve this completely, but the striving for such achievement is in itself a part of the liberation and a foundation for inner security.*

Albert Einstein

My upbringing was pretty wonderful, being born in the '50s. Oldest of three girls. These were the times when children were allowed to be children. We got bruised, made go-carts, and used Dad's tools to build things, with the occasional accident which was quickly patched and kissed. We lived on a ranch in Lakeview Terrace, California, just north of Los Angeles, where my father raised farm animals to make the dollars stretch as far as possible. As children our lives were filled with fresh fruit from the trees on our property, runs through the sprinklers, hikes to the local creek to play with pollywogs, riding horses in the mountains around our home and playing with the neighbor kids. The best part I recall was making friends with the farm animals. I had names for them all and we adored one another. My father warned us not to get attached, but we were young children. We were naturally drawn to the animals. We had pigs, chickens, cows and horses.

Coming home from school one particular day, I remember vividly walking up to the house and seeing my little piglet friend hanging from the tree in our backyard. Was this the little friend I had taught to come, sit and follow me on a leash? It shocked me so badly that it has affected my choices and my dreams from that time forward. This was when I realized it wasn't ok to eat my friends. When I became conscious that "Thou Shall Not Kill" extended to animals too. I was seven years old.

After this shock and into my teen years I had trouble eating flesh. There was the occasional burger, but I never felt good when I consumed animal products. I had it in my head that something precious had to die to get to that burger. The injustice of killing someone for food never left me.

Most of my young adult life I refrained from eating animals. I began to study everything I could get my hands on in an effort to understand the human body and what effects food had on it. I ate only healing foods. At times I would eat only raw food, occasionally juicing, fasting, using grape cures and colonics, all in an effort to be healthy and clean. I succeeded in remaining very healthy and continued to study all the different aspects of health. It fascinated me that food had such an impact on human health and that eating animals was so unhealthy.

I stumbled upon a book that changed my life. That book was *Diet for a New America*, by John Robbins. I read it and re-read it. It affected me so deeply that to this day, nearly twenty years later, I keep it close by. I learned more about the incredible creatures that share our world with us. How truly lovable and sweet and emotional they can be. And not just the ones I grew up with, but dolphins, turtles, and all animals. How they save human lives when the opportunity or need, arises. I realized that I wasn't crazy in feeling bad when eating them; that I wasn't an outcast because I chose to refrain; that there were many other people in the world who felt the same way.

My true awakening came when I stumbled into the world of factory farming. This discovery touched down into my heart and soul and tugged as hard as possible. The research I began to do was haunting me, and so disturbing that I couldn't eat or sleep for months at a time. I began reading, watching videos and even visiting a factory farm at one point. I woke nearly every night in the wee hours hearing baby cows crying for their mothers, chickens screaming and trying to find a little space to call their own. Baby pigs came to me too. I cried with them, blessed them, prayed for them, sent them love and promised to do everything in my power to help them. I was horrified. How on God's earth could people actually think that this is acceptable treatment to fellow loving, breathing, sentient creatures who share our world?

I spent the next few years trying to inform the public. I handed out information everywhere I went. I held events, went to events, gave money to every farm animal organization I could find, talked to everyone I knew, but this was entirely too slow for these animals raised for food. They were suffering and dying at a staggering 500,000 animals per hour. I had to do something and I was desperate. I woke up at 3 a.m. knowing that I had to write a book. That was a way to reach a lot of people, a lot more than I had been reaching. Writing was always an emotional release for me and I seriously needed to unleash this anger/hurt/frustration and horrendous desperation I was feeling. I wrote *The Fast Food Craze* in just over six months. I cried nearly every day I was writing and researching. It did release a lot of what was pent up inside of me, but I was still raging. Literally being eaten up by the injustice of it all. Infuriated with all the suffering that these poor little creatures were enduring, every second of every day of their entire lives. I wanted to scream loudly, to run out to every slaughterhouse and factory farm and free them all, to somehow liberate them from their pain, and from the precious suffering eyes looking up at me, the innocent question that still haunts me today, "Why are you doing this to me?"

By the time I finished the book, I had to get serious. This book had to get out and it had to reach millions. I didn't care about making money, I didn't care what it cost. I mortgaged my home in an effort to pay for the costs involved in self-publishing. I spent the next few years begging God to help me to get this message out. I knew that in all of my research and health experiments, if I hadn't stumbled across this until recently, most of the public hadn't either! I just knew without a doubt that if others knew of this horror, they wouldn't be partaking in it.

My life has changed a lot during the course of these years putting this message out there. I began a radio show called *Wake Up America* in an effort to further reach the "unknowing" public. In hosting this show, interviewing and reading all of my guests' books, I learned more than I could have learned in an institution about animals and their rights.

My major transformation came from one author in particular: Andrew Linzey, who is an author of several books, but one in particular reached me, titled *Animal Gospel*. It was in reading this book that I realized something very profound. I learned that rage and frustration are negative energies. That the only way to truly help other living beings was with the most powerful energy there is available to us. Love. After many struggles I finally learned that in loving everything and everyone, and mostly the ones who did harm, I could actually effect change. That loving them out of their darkness was the only way to show them the way to the light.

As quoted by Andrew Linzey in *Animal Gospel*, Fyodor Dostoevsky said, "...we must not hate those who hate God's world. By doing so we simply push them farther into their own abyss and spiritual darkness... So I don't want to hate anybody, even vivisectors, butchers, trappers, factory farmers, and bullfighters. On the contrary, I want to love them so much that they will not find time, or have the inclination to hunt, and kill, and destroy and maim God's good creatures. I refuse to give those who exploit animals another good reason for not believing in a God of love." (1) I deeply understand this now, and it has opened doors to me that I never believed existed. Mostly, I feel at peace. I feel love for every tree, every mountain, every human being and every precious animal. Here is where true change will come.

I want to share what I have learned with you. *The Missing Peace* will get you there—where we all, as one, need to be to save our world, our animals, and ourselves.

# PART TWO

## Teachers of Health and Inner Peace

Part II uncovers the rarely heard wisdom of both ancient and modern teachers regarding how important our relationship to animals is to our inner peace and to peace in the world. It also offers a summary of some cutting edge health research as well as a look at some of the benefits vegan living brings to the environment and to the world's hungry people.

In Chapter Thirteen, Wisdom from the Past, and Chapter Fourteen, Modern Teachers of Peace and Joy, we discuss such extraordinary people as Gandhi, Jesus Christ, da Vinci, Einstein and many others who felt strongly about the treatment of animals, vegetarianism and the ethic of doing no harm. These chapters help to explain why the people who have told their stories in Part I benefited spiritually from their decision to include animals in their circle of compassion.

Chapter Fifteen, Benefits and Concerns, reviews some research that shows how a diet without animal products can improve our health and that of the planet. Many physicians, scientists and researchers have made the study of plant-based diets their life's work. In addition, we review the devastating role that animal agriculture plays in causing environmental devastation and world hunger. When we adopt a plant-based diet, we gain a sense of serenity and purpose in knowing we are helping to ease these global crises.

Finally, in Chapter Sixteen, Our Shared Vision, we hope to illustrate that each one of us can indeed make a difference and help bring peace to ourselves and to the world.

# CHAPTER THIRTEEN

# Wisdom from the Past

*All beings tremble before violence. All fear death. All love life.*
*See yourself in others. Then whom can you hurt?*
*What harm can you do?*
Buddha

One day at a conference, I (Judy) sat down to a vegan lunch with Bob and Joan, two other attendees whom I was meeting for the first time. What I learned about Bob that day was one of the inspirations for this book. I learned that they had both been seriously ill with various maladies and had gone to an alternative healing clinic after the many doctors they had seen were unable to help them. At this clinic they were taught that what you eat has a huge impact on your physical health.

The food served at the clinic was vegan, but nobody called it that. It was referred to as a cleansing diet. And sure enough, both of them felt so much better in such a short time that they committed to eat that way for the rest of their lives. It was later that they learned that another name for their diet was "vegan".

But it was what Bob told me about his emotions that really grabbed my attention. He said that, while they were healing and eating in this new way, they hadn't thought much about animals or the fact that they were not causing their deaths. That came later. What came first for Bob was a noticeable increase in his compassion, altruism, and empathy. He told me that he had maintained the typical macho male persona for all his adult life, but after he had been on the plant-based diet for a few weeks, he noticed he was tearing up at movies that normally only brought tears to Joan's eyes. Many other similar events took place as well that indicated to him that his heart was opening to others. What a shock and surprise this was for him.

In my studies of spiritual teachers, mystics, and yogis, I was aware that many of them taught their students and followers that they could not fully achieve God consciousness as long as they ate animals. And here was a gentleman who came across this divine compassion by coming in a different doorway—seeking physical healing and finding, in addition to that, a new sense of connection with the people and animals around him.

It was clear to these teachers that human beings are capable of transcending their tendency to commit violent acts against each other, nature, and animals. They believed that it is our destiny as a species to recognize that we are beings of light and to take part in creating a paradise on earth. If only we could rise above our fears, we could become blessings upon the earth instead of perpetrators and victims of endless wars and suffering.

During the many centuries gone by, these wise beings have left their indelible marks both in written and oral history. The good news is that, in this new millennium their teachings are receiving new and much more widespread understanding.

Let's take a look at these teachings that have so faithfully pointed the way we may go if we would only choose to do so. Common to all of them is the abiding insight and ethic that we must do no harm to any living being and that we cannot attain pure consciousness and inner peace as long as we are harming others. This leads naturally to a plant-based diet and a life dedicated to simplicity and nonviolence.

The wisdom that is reviewed here helps to explain and validate the experiences of the people who have shared their stories in Part I. They are not alone in their awakenings, and are, in fact, in very good company.

## Hinduism

The words of the *Bhagavad Gita* are those of an avatar or spiritual teacher by the name of Bhagavan Krishna, according to Paramahansa Yogananda. (1) This ancient Indian scripture is a dialogue between Lord Krishna and his disciple Arjuna. Krishna taught, through this dialogue, about the inner battle that we all experience between our compassionate and violent tendencies.

The *Gita* is a profound spiritual guide for union with God and attaining joy and peace in everyday life. Because ahimsa is an intrinsic part of these teachings, vegetarianism and kindness to all beings is understood as a necessary part of seeking God. As it is written in the *Gita*, "One is dearest to God who has no enemies among the living beings, who is nonviolent to all creatures." The great M.K. Gandhi, who was vegetarian, loved the *Gita* and said of it, "Those who will meditate on the *Gita* will derive fresh joy and new meanings from it every day. There is not a single spiritual tangle which the *Gita* cannot unravel."

Another of the many references that can be found in sacred Hindu texts that supports this spiritual approach is found in the Yajur Veda (12.32), where it is stated that "You must not use your God-given body for killing God's creatures, whether they be humans or animals."

## Zoroastrianism

Zoroastrianism is an ancient religion that some believe promoted both vegetarianism and living simply and in harmony with the earth. Although the name Zarathustra referred, in general, to the many great Zoroastrian teachers, most often the name brings to mind the Zarathustra who may have lived around the 600 BCE. Although there is controversy among scholars regarding when he lived and what he taught, some have concluded that he encouraged his followers to be vegetarian. (2)

At the 13th International Vegetarian Congress meeting in 1953 in Sweden, Dastur Bode, a High Priest of the Zoroastrian religion, explained that the Zoroastrian religion taught the unity and sacredness of life many centuries before Christ. The Christian commandment "Thou shalt not kill", he explained, originated in Zoroastrian teachings.

Many Zoroastrians live in India and, in speaking about India, he noted that at one time, it was totally vegetarian for religious reasons. To this day, many families can trace their vegetarianism back 2,000 to 3,000 years. He urged his audience to learn not to exploit God's creation. Animals, he said, are not to be killed, but protected. Bode made it clear, "If we can feel equally for each one, however low in the scale of consciousness, we shall turn the earth into a paradise." (3)


## Pythagoras

Pythagoras was a Greek mathematician, mystic, scientist, and founder of Pythagoreanism. He is best known for the Pythagorean theorem. Also known as the father of numbers, Pythagoras made influential contributions to religion, music, and philosophy. He called himself a philosopher or lover of wisdom.

His followers, the Pythagoreans, pursued wisdom for its own sake. Materialism, meat eating and wearing clothing made of animal skins were taboo in their society, because they felt it interfered with the attainment of pure contemplation and the practice of non-violence. (4) They studied mathematics and theorized that its principles were the basis of all things. (5)

Aristotle and others described Pythagoras as a supernatural

figure and believed that he could communicate with animals and plants. (6) Although his writings have been lost, Dicaerchus, a pupil of Aristotle, did attempt to record Pythagoras' teachings, and his documents are considered by many to be accurate. Dicaerchus wrote that the Pythagoreans believed that the soul is immortal and that it migrates between humans, plants and animals. Therefore, it followed that in killing and eating creatures, they could be killing their friends and relatives. As a result, they developed a set of proscriptions against eating animals, and they believed such a practice would help them maintain a purity of soul. (7)

During the following century, Socrates and Plato, who were influenced by Pythagoras, continued to carry the same message of nonviolence toward all beings. They assured their students that their astounding spiritual, physical, and intellectual prowess depended in large part on their vegetarian diet and their insistence on doing no harm to any earthling. (8) Pythagoras has often been quoted as saying, "For as long as men massacre animals, they will kill each other. Indeed, he who sows the seed of murder and pain cannot reap joy and love."

## Buddhism

Siddhartha Gautama was born into a warrior caste. Because his father was a rajah who ruled over a kingdom, Gautama was a prince with access to a great fortune. Yet he abandoned this wealth and power to embark on a spiritual quest. After many years of spiritual seeking, he became the Buddha, which means "enlightened one" in Sanskrit.

There is some controversy among scholars regarding the Buddha's actual words. Like Jesus, it took many years (in the Buddha's case, about 500) before his words were set down on paper. Nevertheless, it is agreed by most, if not all Buddhists, that his message was about compassion for all, including people of low castes, women, and animals. Beautiful words attributed to the Buddha are, "To become vegetarian is to step into the stream which leads to Nirvana." (9)

Bhante Henepola Gunaratna, abbot of the Bhavana Society, teaches that "Cultivating the thoughts of non-harm and non-injury and abstinence from killing any living being are so crucial for an individual's peace, harmony, serenity, contentment and attaining liberation from suffering that the Buddha included these principles in the Noble Eightfold Path..." (10)

From the *Surangama Sutra*, we read, "...in seeking to escape from suffering ourselves, why should we inflict it upon others? How can a bhikshu [monk] who hopes to become a deliverer of others, himself be living on the flesh of other sentient beings?" Also in this Buddhist text, we find these words, "If we eat the flesh of living creatures, we are destroying the seeds of compassion." (11)

## Jainism

Interestingly, the great Jain teacher Mahavira was born during the same era as Zarathustra, Pythagoras and Buddha. All of them were devoted to bringing humanity the same message of love and nonviolence.

Then, as now, countless animals, women, children, and men with little power were being subjected to slavery, torture, sacrifice, and endless wars. Many anthropologists and philosophers attribute this great travail to the invention of animal agriculture. This appears to have taken place around 10,000 years ago. From the first hunter's idea of keeping an animal confined in order that he or she be made easier to kill, came the realization that one could not only keep one but several, breed those, and grow an entire herd. But herds require land, and the drive to acquire more land and animals led inexorably to war. (12)

The message, then, of mercy and compassion that was beginning to be heard was certainly needed then as it is now.

Jainism itself may very well be, as its followers maintain, the parent religion of Buddhism and Hinduism and, perhaps, one of the oldest religions. When one examines the teachings of Jesus Christ, one is struck by the strong similarity between some of his words and the teachings of Jainism. Perhaps primitive Christianity also had a bit of Jainism at its roots.

Mahavira was the 24th Jain Tirthankara or enlightened teacher of Jainism. He was born Prince Vardhamana Nataputta. Like the Buddha, he renounced his family's wealth and power to seek enlightenment. He became the enlightened Mahavira, which means "the great man" at the age of 42, through the practice of ahimsa. Ahimsa, of course, means a life devoted to others, to nonviolence, and certainly to doing no harm to any creature. Vegetarianism is a supremely important part of the practice. (13)

Along with his contemporaries, he taught that one could not acquire self-purification or inner peace as long as one was a perpetrator of harm to others, including animals.

## Taoism

The Taoist scripture, the *Tao Te Ching* may have been written as early as the 6th century BCE. Many scholars consider the author to be Lao Tzu. The aim of the book was to influence an end to the wars and violence in China. In the scripture, an enlightened ruler is portrayed as governing through effortless action and nonviolence. The personal reward for taking on such a contemplative approach to ruling would be ecstasy and a long peace-filled life, perhaps even immortality. The Three Jewels or basic virtues of Taoism are compassion, moderation, and humility.

The *Tao Te Ching* has an increasingly broad appeal to millions of lay people, monks and nuns in these modern times. Many of these devoted followers of Taoism are vegetarian, because that is consistent with the Three Jewels and nonviolent way of the Tao. Taoist teachings are consistent with a cruelty-free diet and life, because such practices enhance meditation, health, and spiritual peace. (14)

## Christianity

We can see, then, that a great deal of groundwork was laid prior to the birth of Jesus. While abominable violence raged throughout the world at the hands of human beings, the teachings of those who came before him, as well as their many students, provided another option for humanity. They proposed the radical idea that our species was actually capable of living on the earth as benefactors rather than as destroyers.

Similarly, Jesus' profound teachings were pleas to all people to wake up, stop living in fear of each other, love one another, hold all God's creation sacred, and live simply and completely nonviolently. Rather than "an eye for an eye", he taught "turning the other cheek".

It is strange that we have no uncontestable quotes from Jesus calling for an end to the eating of animals. However, there are many scholars who have found some evidence that he may possibly have been vegetarian and taught nonviolence to animals. According to Keith Akers, author of *The Lost Religion of Jesus*, there were Jewish sects prior to Jesus' birth that held some Pythagorean values, including nonviolence, vegetarianism and simple living. It is possible that Jesus and his Jewish family belonged to such a sect.

Norm Phelps points out in his *Dominion of Love* that, according to the ancient writings of Eusebius, Jesus' brother James was vegan. He was known as "James the Just" partly because he ate no animals and wore no animal skins or wool. This James was the leader of the Christian community after Jesus' crucifixion. Phelps notes that just because James was vegan does not guarantee that Jesus was as well. It could have been a special vow that only James took. "What is certain," states Phelps, "is that in Jesus' family, veganism—even to the extent of not wearing wool clothing—was seen as a sign of righteousness and the epitome of ethical conduct." (15)

Among the apostles, Peter, Thomas, and Matthew were vegetarian. In addition, the early Jewish followers of Jesus, the Ebionites, were vegetarians, according to Epiphanius, author of the 380 CE work, *The Panarion*. Phelps tells us that "Unlike the later gentile Christians, who followed the teachings of St. Paul, the Ebionites learned their practices directly from Jesus, and so their lifestyle reflected his guidance and example." (16)

The beliefs of the Ebionites included vegetarianism, rejection of animal sacrifice, simple living, condemnation of warfare and violence, and Jesus as the true prophet. (17) It certainly seems probable then that their true prophet and beloved teacher, Jesus, was the source of these values and the reason for their fidelity to that lifestyle and faith. Because so many of them attempted to be nonviolent to all creatures and certainly to not eat them, we are challenged to at least consider the possibility that they were following Jesus' example.

As Akers explains, "...it is indisputable that there were large numbers of vegetarians in early Christianity. In fact, there are hardly any references to any early Christians eating meat. The view that Jesus ate meat creates a paradox: vegetarianism was practiced by the apostles and numerous early followers of Jesus, including Jesus' own brother, but not by Jesus himself? It is as if everyone in the early church understood the message but not the messenger. The much more likely explanation is that the original tradition was vegetarian, but that under the pressure of expediency and the popularity of Paul's writings in the second century, vegetarianism was first dropped as a requirement..." (18)

Certainly, no one asserts that Jesus taught violence, animal sacrifice, hatred, or killing. It is difficult to imagine that a teacher such as he, whose message was that God is Love and that we are all to love one another, could condone the horrific torture and slaughter of innocent animals. Even the cosmic image of him as an infant in a stable causes us to ponder his relationship with animals. After all, the animals were among the very few privileged to be with him at this birth and to surround him with their peaceful presence.

Reverend Professor Andrew Linzey, in referring to Luke 12:6, states "...I hazard a guess that what Jesus was implying by saying that God remembered even the smallest, cheapest birds [sold] in the market was that we would see (and do) it all differently if we really saw them as God sees them." (19)

Jesus incurred great wrath from the merchants and priests by interfering with the selling and sacrificial slaughtering of innocent animals in what was supposed to be a holy temple dedicated to God. Jesus knew God to be a loving, nurturing presence, not a distant, vengeful God who demanded violent, bloody sacrifices of helpless creatures.

Some scholars believe that it was Jesus' daring attempt to stop the sacrifices in the temple that was the final straw that led to his crucifixion. After all, that temple ritual was a source of tremendous wealth and power to those who organized it.

Author Rynn Berry believes he has found cogent evidence for Jesus' having been a vegetarian, and an animal liberationist. Berry states, "To me Jesus' life follows the arc of a persecuted animal liberator, who is brought up on charges and condemned to death after risking his life to free the sacrificial animals from the Temple." (20)

As was stated above, many followers of Jesus lived on plants alone in apparent imitation of him. In the paragraphs that follow, we will find more examples of that.

## The Message Lives On

There have been, from ancient times to the present, those who have managed to hold a vision of what life on earth is supposed to be. In spite of the degradation and violence on earth, they have maintained their faith that human beings could create a world of peace, a paradise. They have dedicated their lives to discovering how that could happen, and that heroic effort has sustained us all throughout the centuries in more ways than we can ever know.

These visionaries number in the millions. It would take volumes to name each one and describe their tireless work that has so profoundly benefited us and the animals. Their plant-based diets and kindness to animals were a consistent and essential part of their efforts to live from a higher consciousness and demonstrate that we all have access to the divine within.

**Plutarch** was a Greek philosopher, historian, and biographer born in 46 CE. He once stated in defense of animals and of vegetarianism, "It is certainly not lions and wolves that we eat out of self-defense; on the contrary, we ignore these and slaughter harmless, tame creatures without stings or teeth to harm us, creatures that, I swear, Nature appears to have produced for the sake of their beauty and grace. But nothing abashed us...not the cleanliness of their habits or the unusual intelligence that may be found in the poor wretches. No, for the sake of a little flesh we deprive them of sun, of light, of the duration of life to which they are entitled by birth and being." (21)

**Leonardo da Vinci** was born in Vinci, Italy in 1452. He was an inventor and a man of multiple talents, including art, mathematics, science, engineering, architecture, botany, writing, and music. The author of *Art Through the Ages*, Helen Gardner, wrote, "The scope and depth of his interests were without precedent. His mind and personality seem to us as superhuman, the man himself, mysterious and remote." It has been said of him that he is the greatest painter and most talented person who has ever lived. (22)

Giorgio Vasari described Leonardo in this way, "In the normal course of events many men and women are born with remarkable talents; but occasionally, in a way that transcends nature, a single person is marvelously endowed by Heaven with beauty, grace and talent in such abundance that he leaves other men far behind, all his actions seem inspired and indeed everything he does clearly comes from God rather than from human skill. Everyone acknowledged that this was true of Leonardo da Vinci, an artist of outstanding physical beauty, who displayed infinite grace in everything that he did and who cultivated his genius so brilliantly that all problems he studied he solved with ease." (23)

Vasari noted also that Leonardo had a deep respect for all life and was occasionally observed buying caged birds in the marketplace and setting them free. In addition, this famous artist was a vegetarian and was quoted as saying, "The time will come when men such as I will look upon the murder of animals as they now look on the murder of men."

**Guru Nanak** was the founder of Sikhism in the fifteenth century. He considered flesh eating antithetical to a spiritual life. The Sikh 3HO (happy, healthy, holy) Golden Temple movement remains vibrant today and is totally vegetarian.

**Benjamin Franklin**, American statesman, scientist and author, was born in 1706. He helped draft the Declaration of Independence. As ambassador to France, he negotiated an alliance with France and a peace settlement with Britain. As a scientist he is especially well known for his research in electricity.

In his autobiographical *Self Improvement Plan*, he wrote that he did not eat meat and that a vegetarian diet was healthier than a diet filled with meat. He also noted that, since meat was more expensive than plant foods, he had more money to buy books.

**One Hundred and Fifty Vegetarian Christian Saints.** Christianity has a legacy of many saints, and even one pope (St. Peter Celestine), who were committed to a cruelty-free diet and lifestyle. While many popes and bishops waged war and amassed great fortunes, there were many Christian men and women who lived as they believed Jesus lived.

To them, the values he imparted were arrayed around the central teaching of loving God and loving one another. Simple living, not taking more than one needs, serving others, loving all creation, kindness, total nonviolence, inner peace—all these led naturally to and, in fact, necessitated a nonviolent diet and a refusal to view animals as here for the use of human beings.

Dr. Holly Roberts, in her book *Vegetarian Christian Saints*, tells the stories of 150 saints, who have been canonized by the Catholic Church. From the early first century until the present, they sought and found the "peace that passes all understanding", and dining only on plant foods was an intrinsic part of their peace.

Within the pages of her book, we find the story of St. Clare of Rimini, who was born in 1265. Although her Italian family was wealthy, she felt called to devote her life to others. There was much illness where she lived, and she cared for the sick, helping all in need. At one point she heard about a man whose hand was going to be chopped off. She sold herself into slavery in order to get the money needed to save him from his fate. She wished to inflict no harm on any of God's beloved creation and so ate only a plant-based diet. (24)

St. Anselm, born in Italy in 1033, became an archbishop who

taught his students to live simple lives without anger and greed and without harming others, including animals. One day he was on a road when hunters rode by on horseback following their dogs who were close to catching a hare. Anselm told the dogs not to hurt the hare. When he did, the dogs surrounded their intended prey and began to lick her affectionately. Nevertheless, the hunters moved toward the animal to kill her, but the saint said to them, "For the poor unhappy creature there is nothing to laugh at or be glad; its mortal foes are about it, and it flies to us for life." Chastened by the saint's sincerity, the hunters left the hare unharmed. (25) This is no mere legend, as Archbishop Anselm's secretary was a witness to this event and duly recorded it for posterity.

St. Clare of Assisi was well known, as was her beloved friend, St. Francis, for her love for all creatures. Her love necessitated vegetarianism, of course. Roberts described St. Clare by saying she "lived without consuming flesh so as to share the privilege of life with all God's creatures". (26)

**John Wesley** founded the Methodist Church in the 1700s. He was a vegetarian, and spoke out in his sermons about animal suffering. "Nothing is more sure," he preached, "than that as 'the Lord is loving to every man', so 'his mercy is over all his works';...both wild and domesticated animals are exposed to the violence and cruelty of him that is now their common enemy—man...[This] may encourage us to imitate Him whose mercy is over all His works...not one of them is forgotten in the sight of our Father which is in heaven." (27)

**The 1800s.** Of course, vegetarianism continued to flourish in the East during the 1800s. Meanwhile in the West, although vegetarian philosophy and the concept of animal rights was not as widespread, nevertheless, some of the most notable and influential people in history continued to teach its spiritual, health, and ethical importance.

Such well-known individuals included: Johnny Appleseed, who considered it a sin to kill any animal for food, and George Bernard Shaw, famed essayist and dramatist.

Great vegetarian religious leaders included: William Metcalfe, who founded the Bible-Christian Church in the U.S. and believed, as his minister son explained, "there is a desolation wrought in the soul by the sin of flesh eating;" Annie Besant, famous Theosophist and social reformer; William and Catherine Booth, co-founders of the Salvation Army; Bronson Alcott, leader of New England transcendentalism and father of famous author, Louisa May Alcott; and Ellen White, founder of the Seventh Day Adventist Church, who stated, "Think of the cruelty to animals that meat eating involves and its effect on those who inflict and those who behold it. How it destroys the tenderness with which we should regard these creatures of God!"

This historical overview is included in order to help validate the discoveries of the folks who have shared their stories in this book. With the support of the wise mystics, saints, and teachers of the past, we learn that it is not unusual at all to obtain more joy and bliss, to obtain heaven within, as a result of living a life dedicated to nonviolence toward all beings.

*And in the end, the love you take is equal to the love you make.*
*The Beatles*

# Modern Teachers of Peace and Joy

*Vegetarianism is a major step on the road to world peace;*
*as long as human beings will go on shedding the blood of animals,*
*there will never be any peace...there will be no justice*
*as long as man will stand with a knife or with a gun*
*and destroy those who are weaker than he is.*
Isaac Bashevis Singer, 1978 Nobel Prize in Literature

In 2008 Oprah Winfrey hosted Eckhart Tolle on her TV show and shared his teachings online as well. Tolle's work goes beyond the usual self-help television guests who help people sort through marital and parental problems. He is sharing ancient wisdom that for centuries interested only a rare few. This is a different time. The desire for awakening to higher consciousness appears to be rising among human beings at an unprecedented rate.

Tolle, along with many of the other spiritual teachers of today, understands that we have arrived, as a species, at an evolutionary turning point. We are being given the chance to take the leap into an entirely new level of consciousness. There is not a lot of time. Obviously, we cannot walk much farther along the destructive path that we are currently on and expect the earth to be able to support us.

The teachers featured in this chapter continue the work of revealing to humanity that nonviolent living is a primary key to the healing of the planet and of ourselves.

**Charles and Myrtle Fillmore** founded the Unity School of Christianity. Charles wrote often and passionately about the physical, mental, social, and spiritual harmfulness of eating any food derived from animals. He and Myrtle believed that anyone who wished to develop spiritual maturity must live and eat nonviolently. He wrote, "I can say about flesh eating that the Spirit has shown me repeatedly that I could not refine my body and make it a harmonious instrument for the soul, so long as I continued to fill it with the cells of dead animals...We need never look for universal peace on this earth until men stop killing animals for food. The lust for blood has permeated the race thought and the destruction of life will continue to repeat its psychology the world round, until men willingly observe the law in all phases of life, 'Thou shalt not kill.'" (1)

He taught that our love "must flow forth in protecting streams when any creature is in danger of violence or destruction". (2) Yet he and Myrtle saw that in the world at large people continued to consume the very thing that made it so difficult to feel that love within. Instead, they noted, "...our vague fears, our difficulty sleeping, our dread of the future are very likely emanating from the bodies of the animals who were brutally killed while absolutely terrified and now lie decomposing in our stomachs". Although the word "vegan" had not yet been coined, the Fillmores understood the concept of pure vegetarianism and a nonviolent lifestyle. For example, the Unity Bibles which they published were covered with a non-leather material.

Sadly, while many of the valuable Unity teachings did spread around the world, this very important and foundational piece of the Fillmores' teachings went missing. It is rare indeed to find a Unity Church that has honored this simple mandate to live without violence to animals.

**Paramahansa Yogananda**, Indian teacher of yoga and spiritual ideals, was invited to the U.S. to give a talk to an interfaith congress of religious leaders in 1920. Ultimately he decided to make his home in America and became known as the father of yoga in the West. Eventually, he established the Self-Realization Fellowship with headquarters in California. He felt divinely inspired to share the beauty and value of meditation with people of all religions and to teach the divinity of the human spirit.

His presence in the U.S. helped further an understanding that there were common threads of truth woven through all religions. These shared ideas included the importance of universal love and peace for all creation and the very real possibility of humanity giving up its violent ways and creating the peaceful paradise that lives in all our dreams. Yogananda, of course, was vegetarian and boldly predicted that the U.S. would be completely vegetarian by the year 2050.

**Mohandas K. Gandhi**, Indian political and spiritual leader, led India to independence from British rule. He used nonviolent civil disobedience, which he called satyagraha, to accomplish this. He is commonly known around the world as Mahatma or Great Soul. In India he is considered the Father of the Nation. His birthday, October 2nd, is celebrated as the International Day of Non-Violence.

Gandhi lived modestly, was vegetarian, and wore traditional Indian clothing. His simple living and vegetarianism were part of his commitment to self-purification. His social protests often involved long fasts. (3)

Gandhi is considered one of the great sages of the world. When he was alive, Indians showered their love, respect and devotion on him in an unprecedented measure. They thronged his way to have a glimpse of him, to hear one word from his lips. They applied the dust from the paths he walked to their foreheads. For them, he was almost an incarnation of God who had come to break the chains of their slavery. The whole world bowed to him in reverence. Even his opponents held him in great respect. (4)

Gandhi's message of universal love, peace and non-violence was consistent with his vegetarianism. He once said, "The greatness of a nation and its moral progress can be judged by the way its animals are treated." He also declared, "I do feel that spiritual progress does demand at some stage that we should cease to kill our fellow creatures for the satisfaction of our bodily wants." And, "To my mind the life of a lamb is no less precious than that of a human being. I should be unwilling to take the life of a lamb for the sake of the human body. I hold that, the more helpless a creature, the more entitled it is to the protection by man from the cruelty of man." (5)

**Leo Tolstoy**, a Russian count, is considered to be one of the greatest novelists who ever lived. His masterpieces, *War and Peace* and *Anna Karenina*, are still read in high schools and universities today. Tolstoy is also known as a humanitarian, peace activist, and philosopher.

Gandhi and Martin Luther King, Jr. were profoundly influenced by Tolstoy's ideas on nonviolent resistance, expressed in such works as *The Kingdom of God is Within You*. (6)

In 1908 his "Letter to a Hindu" was published in an Indian newspaper. (7) In reaction to the article, Gandhi began a correspondence with Tolstoy. He acknowledged his debt to Tolstoy in his autobiography, calling Tolstoy "the greatest apostle of non-violence that the present age has produced". (8) In addition to non-violent resistance, they were both vegetarian. (9)

"Not long ago I had a talk with a retired soldier," wrote Tolstoy in his essay, "The First Step", "and he was surprised at my assertion that it was a pity to kill animals for food, and said the usual things about it's being ordained. But afterwards he agreed with me: 'Especially when they are quiet, tame cattle. They come, poor things, trusting you. It is very pitiful.'" (10)

He went on to say, "Such a situation is dreadful. Not the suffering and death of the animals, but that man suppresses in himself unnecessarily, the highest spiritual capacity—that of sympathy and pity towards living creatures—and by violating his own feelings, becomes cruel. And how deeply seated in the human heart is the injunction not to take life. But by the assertion that God ordained the slaughter of animals, and above all as a result of habit, people entirely lose their natural feeling." (11)

According to Tolstoy, "Thou shalt not kill, does not apply to murder of one's own kind only, but to all living beings; and this Commandment was inscribed in the human breast long before it was proclaimed from Sinai."

He spent the last twenty-five years of his life living as a peasant and eating very simply on bread, porridge, fruits, and vegetables. In explaining how vegetarianism contributes to one's compassion and morality, Tolstoy made this statement in "The First Step", "I only wish to say that for a good life a certain order of good actions is indispensable; that if a man's aspirations toward right living be serious they will inevitably follow one definite sequence; and that in this sequence the first virtue a man will strive after will be self-control, self-restraint. And in seeking for self-control a man will inevitably follow one definite sequence, and in this sequence the first thing will be self-control in food—fasting. And in fasting, if he be really and seriously seeking to live a good life, the first thing from which he will abstain will always be the use of animal food, because, to say nothing of the excitation of the passions caused by such food, its use is simply immoral, as it involves the performance of an act which is contrary to the moral feeling—killing; and is called forth only by greediness and the desire for tasty food."

**Thich Nhat Hanh**, a Zen monk from Vietnam, is known by his students as Thay (or teacher). Years ago he and Martin Luther King, Jr. agreed it was necessary to oppose the Vietnam War publicly and thus empower and build the peace movement in the U.S.

He continues his work in peace and social justice and is dearly loved by people all over the world. His many books, poetry, workshops, and retreats have helped awaken humanity to the higher consciousness needed for survival on the planet. He has also spoken out publicly on behalf of animals and the importance of veganism for the accomplishment of world peace, inner peace, and indeed saving humanity itself from destruction.

In a "Letter from Thay" dated October 12, 2007, he wrote of many reasons why veganism is important. Because 40,000 children die of starvation every day while 80% of corn and 95% of oats in the U.S. are fed to livestock, he explained, "Eating meat and drinking alcohol with mindfulness, we will realize that we are eating the flesh of our own children."

Referring to the United Nations report, "Livestock's Long Shadow: Environmental Issues and Options", (12) he reported that the livestock industry is one of the top two or three biggest contributors to the destruction of land, pollution of water and air, water shortages, and loss of habitat.

"We are vegetarian," he wrote, "with the intention to nourish our compassion towards the animals. Now we also know that we eat vegetarian in order to protect the earth...Thay [he refers to himself in the third person] believes that it is not so difficult to stop eating meat, when we know that we are saving the planet by doing so."

Referring to a report that concluded, "You could spend more than $20,000 on a Prius and still emit 50 percent more carbon dioxide than you would if you just gave up eating meat and other animal products," (13) Thay said "Being vegetarian is already enough to save the world. Who amongst us has not experienced the delicious taste of vegetarian foods? Only when we are too used to eating meat we cannot see this truth."

In his October letter, Thay promised his students that all his retreats and practice centers worldwide would be vegan from that day forward. "Our present practice is to help everyone become aware of the danger of global warming, in order to help save Mother Earth and all species. We know that if there is no collective awakening, then the earth and all species will not have a chance to be saved. Our daily life has to show that we are awake." (14)

The Dalai Lama spoke at a World Peace conference in India in 2006. At the conference all the food served to the 200,000 attendees was vegetarian. In his speech at the conference, he criticized factory farming, meat consumption, and the trade of wild animal skins and furs.

He went on to say, "If the human community is based on principles of peace, it will lessen the sufferings caused to millions and billions of animals. Otherwise, out of humans' limitless and unjustified greed and desires, they build beef farms, pig farms, and fish farms which never existed before and are not needed. And now, when the animals bring diseases they are killed in large numbers. So many fishes are killed and they suffer so much.

"These days there are many Tibetan groups in India working for vegetarianism and spreading compassion for animals, such acts are extremely good and something to rejoice. Most of the monasteries have also turned their kitchens vegetarian which is really good." (15)

**Albert Einstein** is perhaps best known for his theory of relativity and for his 1921 Nobel Prize in Physics. (16) Nuclear energy, quantum physics, big bang theory, and basic electronics all bear his imprint.

In 1999, Einstein was named "Person of the Century" by *Time* magazine. A Gallup poll rated him as the fourth most admired person of the 20th century. According to "The 100: A Ranking of the Most Influential Persons in History", Einstein was "the greatest scientist of the twentieth century and one of the supreme intellects of all time". (17)

Einstein was part of the Ethical Culture movement, which is premised on the idea that honoring and living in accordance with ethical principles is central to what it takes to live meaningful lives and to create a world that is good for all. The movement believed that ethics are at the heart of all religions. (18)

Einstein believed vegetarianism was the ethical way to live, as evidenced by his own statement: "… it is my view that a vegetarian manner of living by its purely physical effect on the human temperament would most beneficially influence the lot of mankind". (19)

Einstein's belief in compassion and kindness towards all is evidenced in this often quoted statement, "Taken on the whole, I would believe that Gandhi's views were the most enlightened of all the political men in our time. We should strive to do things in his spirit... not to use violence in fighting for our cause, but by non-participation in what we believe is evil."(20)

**Father John Dear** is a Jesuit priest, peace activist, and author of many books, including his most recent, *Transfiguration*. He has served as the director of the Fellowship of Reconciliation, and has dedicated his life to creating a peaceful world.

For years Father John has encouraged people to be vegetarian. He connects his peace work with animal rights by saying that "the only way out of this culture of violence is through the ancient wisdom of nonviolence. I remember what Dr. King said the night before he was assassinated: 'The choice before us is no longer violence or non-violence; it's non-violence or non-existence.'" He believes that to be consistent with Jesus' teachings, we must "side with the poor and oppressed peoples of the world and with animals". (21)

"As a Christian," he wrote in a recent article, "I became a vegetarian because of the Gospel mandate of Matthew 25, 'Whatever you did to the least of these, you did to me'... being vegetarian boils down to peacemaking...'Vegetarianism', Tolstoy wrote, 'is the taproot of humanitarianism.' Other great humanitarians like Mahatma Gandhi, Albert Schweitzer and Thich Nhat Hanh agree. The only diet for a peacemaker is a vegetarian diet." (22)

**Peace Pilgrim** walked more than 25,000 miles speaking out for world peace. She carried only a few possessions and walked until food and shelter was offered to her. She saw veganism as an intrinsic part of her message of peace for all.

**And many others:** A quick glance at a few more modern mystics as well as some recent events may provide more insight into this journey toward peace. For example, Rachel Carson said "We cannot have peace among men, whose hearts delight in killing any living creature. By every act that glorifies or even tolerates such moronic delight in killing, we set back the progress of humanity."

Albert Schweitzer spoke of widening the circle of our compassion to include all living beings and nature. Without doing so, he believed we could never find peace. And eloquently, Dr. Elizabeth Farians declared, "Just as there is no peace without justice, so there is no peace without compassion for every living thing, because the human heart can abide neither injustice nor cruelty."

B.K.S. Iyengar, one of the world's foremost experts on yoga, said,

"A vegetarian diet is essential to the practice of yoga." In 2005, the National Council of Churches, which is a coalition of 36 faith groups representing 45 million Americans, called humanity the "uncreator", and stated that the churches have failed to address the devastation caused by people to the earth and to animals.

In 2008, 59 Unitarian Universalist ministers called upon congregations and colleagues to move toward a plant-based diet. "Recognizing the moral claims of justice, our obligation to future generations, and the oneness of all life, we invite you to join us: vegetarians and vegans for whom conscious food choices have become some of our most important spiritual practices." (23)

Imam Qasim Ahmed, a contemporary Muslim leader, stated that the *Qur'an* leaves no doubt that God sent Mohammed on a mission of mercy for all creation, not just human beings. Ahmed believes that vegetarianism is the spiritual ideal and points out that Mohammed once said "an act of cruelty toward an animal is as bad as an act of cruelty toward a human being". According to Ahmed, the Islamic Holiness, M.R. Bawa Muhaiyaddeen, who many believe to be a saint, practiced vegetarianism. In describing the spiritual seeker, Muhaiyaddeen said, "Inside he will not intend any harm or pain to any other life. Nor will he do anything harmful or eat any life on the outside. This is a state of wisdom, clarity, and the light of God." (24)

Many Jewish people have embraced veganism as a spiritual necessity. Richard Schwartz, professor and author, stated, "A vegetarian diet, by not wasting scarce resources and by not requiring the daily slaughter of helpless creatures of God, is most likely to lead to that day of harmony and peace..." The values of the *Torah*, he quotes Rabbi David Rosen as saying, are "overwhelmingly incompatible with carnivorous indulgence". (25)

In more news of awakening compassion, the National Council for Science and the Environment's 2008 conference on climate change served only vegan fare at the meeting. And one million citizens of Taiwan have pledged to eat a vegan diet for one year. By doing so, they estimate they will reduce carbon emissions by a minimum of 1.5 million tons. (26)

Inspired by Kathy Freston's book *Quantum Wellness*, Oprah Winfrey participated in a 21 day vegan diet. She and Kathy referred to it as a detox diet. Of course, the health benefits of such a diet are impressive, and detoxification is one of them, but on Oprah's first day of her culinary adventure, she addressed the benefit we are studying in this book. Oprah stated that Freston is not only talking about physical wellness, but also about spiritual wellness and integrity. "How can you say you're trying to spiritually evolve, without even a thought about what happens to the animals whose lives are sacrificed in the name of gluttony?" Oprah asked in her "Week One: Sunday Blog".

This consciousness for animals to which we are awakening is indeed a spiritual journey for all humanity and all life. Perhaps one of the reasons that this awareness and compassion is growing among people is because there has been so much exposure in the media and online of the suffering of animals worldwide at the hands of people. Gandhi explained to his followers that the reason they were to suffer and not resist abuse and torture at the hands of their persecutors was because such willingness to suffer would open the hearts of the persecutors and transform them into allies. With each new undercover video and fact-finding mission revealing the unconscionable torture that goes on second by second for billions of animals, the opportunity for the hearts of human beings to open to these innocent earthlings increases.

> *Kindness and compassion towards all living beings*
> *is a mark of a civilized society. Racism, economic deprival...*
> *bullfighting and rodeos are all cut from the same defective fabric:*
> *violence. Only when we have become nonviolent towards*
> *all life will we have learned to live well ourselves.*
> Cesar Chavez, civil rights activist

# CHAPTER FIFTEEN

# Benefits and Concerns

*Nothing will benefit human health and increase
the chances for survival of life on Earth
as much as the evolution to a vegetarian diet.*
Albert Einstein

There are many rewards that are realized by the change to a plant-based diet. Not only does it help us find inner peace, but the health and environmental benefits are enormous. It is gratifying to know that our individual choice to live non-violently can release enough grain and land to feed an estimated 20 people every year, save the lives of over 100 animals annually and significantly reduce the size of our ecological footprint.

Many prominent physicians, scientists, medical researchers and authors, some of whom are mentioned below, have done years of research. Their findings demonstrate that human beings live much healthier lives when they refrain from eating any type of animals or their products.

The pollution crisis facing our world today is strongly related to the destructive impact of animal agribusiness as it affects our rivers, air quality, soil and drinking water.

World hunger is an issue that concerns us all, and in this chapter we illustrate the fact that a large percentage of the world's grain production and water usage goes towards raising animals. This is grain that could feed our starving human population, and, for many, this issue alone is sufficient motivation to change to a plant-based diet.

## Health Benefits

**T. Colin Campbell, Ph.D.** is the co-author of *The China Study.* A 20-year study of the diets and health of over 65,000 individuals ranging from age thirty-five to sixty-four, in and around China, is the basis of this inspiring book. The diets of these subjects were compared to the average American diet. The level of protein and fat consumed by Americans was significantly higher. The study concluded that obesity and a multitude of other health issues in the U.S. are associated with the consumption of too much animal protein.

Dr. Campbell wrote, "One of the most dramatic findings of the China project was the strong association between foods of animal origin and cancer. We found that one of the strongest predictors of Western diseases was blood cholesterol. Lower blood cholesterol levels were linked to lower rates of heart disease, cancer and other Western diseases. As blood cholesterol levels decreased from 170 to 90 ml/dl, cancers of the liver, rectum, colon, lung, breast, stomach, esophagus and brain (in both adults and children) decreased. It is not enough to simply make a few small dietary changes to prevent cancer. A major dietary shift towards plant based foods and away from animal foods is likely to produce much greater benefits."

Dean Ornish, MD, in highly recommending *The China Study*, stated "Everyone in the field of nutrition science stands on the shoulders of Dr. Campbell, who is one of the giants in the field. This is one of the most important books about nutrition ever written—reading it may save your life."

*The China Study's* chapters review the major diseases and their connection to the consumption of animals or their products. Dr. Campbell himself was raised on a farm and was a meat eater most of his life. This study changed his mind. He is now a vegan and lives entirely on a plant-based diet.

**John McDougall, M.D.,** author of *The McDougall Plan* and founder of Dr. McDougall's Health and Medical Center, has helped many individuals regain their health. As he stated on my (Tina's) radio show, *Wake Up America,* "People come in overweight and with bags full of prescription drugs, and leave tremendously thinner, and most, without the need of any further medication."

On his website, drmcdougall.com, the "Star McDougallers" section showcases hundreds of stories of people who have healed themselves. Among these stories is that of Dr. Ruth Heidrich, who cured her breast cancer and osteoporosis by diet alone.

Dr. Heidrich believed at one time that she was eating a healthy diet, which included chicken, fish and low-fat dairy. She was diagnosed with invasive breast cancer, which had spread entirely through her breast, into her bones and one lung. Physicians removed a lump, but the cancer remained.

Instead of choosing chemotherapy and radiation, Dr. Heidrich followed McDougall's plan. Not only did her cancer completely disappear, her bone density increased, eliminating her osteoporosis, and her arthritis was cured. In 1999 she was declared "one of the top ten fittest women in North America". She has run the Ironman Triathlon six times, 67 marathons, and has won over 800 racing trophies—cancer free and on a vegan diet. Dr. Ruth Heidrich is a hero to me. She continues her career and runs marathons as if cancer was just a small bump in the road. She is 67 years old as of this writing, and still going.

Consistent with *The China Study*, the McDougall Program proposes that diets high in starch, such as rice, wheat, potatoes, corn and beans, along with plenty of fruit and vegetables, are found among people who remain slim and healthy their entire lives, such as the Chinese, Japanese, Koreans, and Malaysians. Among these populations, obesity is almost unknown.

According to McDougall, diseases which are often associated with the rich Western diet include allergies, diabetes, heart and kidney problems, hormone imbalances, high blood pressure, osteoporosis, strokes, gastrointestinal disorders, and many forms of cancer. Diet is a primary causative factor of these diseases. Smoking, alcohol, lack of exercise and stress are secondary factors. A primary factor must be present for disease to develop; a secondary factor aggravates the disease process after the development has begun.

Diet and lifestyle changes are the most effective treatment for chronic forms of the diseases listed above—far surpassing in results any drug or surgical therapy, according to McDougall. If you eliminate the cause, then the body's healing mechanisms can take over, resulting in improvement or recovery.

**Caldwell B. Esselstyn, Jr., M.D.**'s latest book, titled *Prevent and Reverse Heart Disease*, is based on the findings of a 20-year study first published in the *American Journal of Cardiology*. The book explains how we can end the heart disease epidemic in our country by changing what we eat. He convincingly argues that a plant-based, oil-free diet can, not only prevent heart disease, but can also stop its progression and reverse its effects.

The patients in Dr. Esselstyn's initial study came to him with advanced coronary artery disease. Within months on his program, their cholesterol levels, angina symptoms and blood flow improved dramatically. Twenty years later they remain symptom and heart disease free.

Many physicians who have been interviewed on Wake Up America have spoken out about the medical community and the lack of interest it often shows in their findings about the importance of diet.

This makes me very sad. The majority of Americans trust the medical industry and its physicians. However, there are many men and women in the fields of medicine and nutrition who have looked beyond the constraints of conventionality and stand as pioneers in their fields. I thank God every day for people of medicine who speak the truth and help people avoid costly or unnecessary medical treatment by teaching the wonders of a plant-based diet. These doctors and nutritionists certainly deserve our respect and gratitude.

## The Pollution Crisis

Animal farming has a bigger carbon footprint than all cars, planes and trucks put together. But, even more staggering is the pollution to our waters, air, and soil. The EPA estimates that over the past ten years, over 35,000 miles of rivers in the United States have been polluted by large-scale feedlots. Ground water in over seventeen states has been contaminated—and all due to giant, corporate owned animal factories, or Concentrated Animal Feeding Operations (CAFO's).

The EPA estimates that CAFO's produce around 500 million tons of manure annually. The disposal practices are not up to date and most manure is sprayed into croplands or stored in open-air pits called lagoons. These lagoons often leak or spill causing pollution to water sources and creating a major health risk to people, wildlife and fish.

Lagoons also emit hundreds of dangerous gasses into the atmosphere, including ammonia, methane, carbon dioxide, nitrogen and hydrogen sulfide. A single lagoon releases millions of bacteria, and most are resistant to antibiotics used for human illnesses.

Spills and emissions aren't the worst thing that can happen to toxic waste lying exposed in fields and lagoons. In 1999 Hurricane Floyd washed 120 million gallons of unsheltered hog waste into the Tar, Neuse, Roanoke, Pamlico, New and Cape Fear rivers. Many of the lagoons of eastern North Carolina were several feet underwater. Satellite photographs showed a dark brown tide closing over the region's waterways and feeding itself out to sea in a long, well-defined channel. Very little freshwater marine life remained behind. Tens of thousands of drowned pigs were strewn across the land. Beaches located miles from these hog lagoons were slathered in feces. A picture taken at the time shows a shark eating a dead pig three miles off the North Carolina coast. (1)

One of the most effective steps toward resolving such overwhelming environmental problems is to drastically reduce or eliminate the consumption of animal products. Once we discover the power we have to stop the devastation, we can become proactive caretakers and healers of the earth, air, water, soil, and all who live here.


## World Hunger

It is estimated that 40 thousand people are dying each day from starvation. This is not how it's supposed to be, and we all know this in our hearts. Animal agriculture is a major culprit in the world hunger crisis.

The Worldwatch Institute states, "In a world where one in every six people goes hungry every day, the politics of meat consumption are increasingly heated, since meat production is an inefficient use of grain—the grain is used more efficiently when consumed directly by humans. Continued growth in meat output is dependent on feeding grains to animals, creating competition for grain between affluent meat eaters and the poor."

The Worldwatch research indicates that more than 40% of all grain grown in the world is fed to animals raised for food. Livestock now eat twice the amount of grain as the entire human population in the United States.

Dr. Walden Bello, Executive Director for the Institute for Food and Development Policy, notes, "Every time you eat a hamburger you are having a relationship with thousands of people you never met. Not just people at the supermarket or fast food restaurant, but possibly World Bank officials in Washington, D.C., and peasants from Central and South America. And many of these people are hungry. The fact is that there is enough food in the world for everyone. But tragically, much of the world's food and land resources are tied up in producing beef and other livestock—food for the well-off—while millions of children and adults suffer from malnutrition and starvation."

Bello further states, "In Central America, staple corn crop production has been replaced by cattle ranching, which now occupies two-thirds of the arable land. The World Bank encouraged this switch-over with an eye toward expanding U.S. fast food and frozen-dinner markets. The resulting expansion of cattle ranching has deprived peasants of access to the land they depend on for growing food. And because of ranching's limited ability to create jobs (cattle ranching creates thirteen times fewer jobs per acre than coffee production), rural hunger has soared. What does this all have to do with our hamburgers? The American fast-food diet and the meat-eating habits of the wealthy around the world support a world food system that diverts food resources from the hungry."

So, while America has its obesity health crisis, millions of mothers cannot feed their starving children. Where is the balance? If we wish to call our world a place of love, we must begin our journey into a non-violent lifestyle.

We can together bring balance to this injustice. Each one of us can have an impact—setting an example for our children and their children, and leaving our world a better place for them.

*May all be fed, May all be healed, May all be loved.*
John Robbins

# Completing the Puzzle:
# Our Shared Vision

*The 18th century gave rights to man; the 19th century gave
rights to slaves; and the 20th century gave rights to women.
The 21st century, I verily believe, will give rights to animals,
and that will be a glorious day in the history of humanity.
I believe there will be no peace on Earth unless we stop all killing.*
Dada J.P. Vaswami

In the great puzzle of life, much has been accomplished. We human
beings have come far in our understanding that we are here to care
for each other and to benefit others. And over the centuries we have
taken many effective steps to eliminate violence to people. Yet, despite these actions, wars, slavery, murder, rape, and torture continue
to rage around the world. Peace continues to elude us.

The personal stories and sacred wisdom shared in this book are inviting us to embrace this one simple statement: we can bring peace to ourselves and other human beings, but only when we end our violence toward animals.

Let us take the necessary steps to give animals their rights to freedom from all human exploitation and end the brutal use and killing of them. This world is meant to be a garden of peace, not a realm of endless suffering.

Could we really create an earthly paradise? Will Tuttle, in his *The World Peace Diet*, described a positive momentum "unquestionably building in spite of the established forces of domination and violent control that would suppress it. Like a birth or metamorphosis, a new mythos [world-view] is struggling through us to arise and replace the obsolete herding [domination] mythos…It is vital that we all contribute to the positive revolution for which our future is calling." (1)

Wendell Berry put it this way: "We must recover the sense of the majesty of creation, and the ability to be worshipful in its presence. For I do not doubt that it is only on the condition of humility and reverence before the world that our species will be able to remain in it." (2)

In a recent article in *Yes!* magazine, David Korten, author of *When Corporations Rule the World* and *The Great Turning*, affirmed that it is basic human nature to care about each other and to want to connect. He asserted that we gain more happiness from caring relationships than from obtaining more material possessions. According to the scientific research he cited, our brains are wired to have sympathy for another's suffering and pleasure when we help others. This affirms Martin Luther King, Jr.'s famous statement, "Let us realize the arc of the moral universe is long but it bends toward justice." The good news is, according to Korten, "The changes we must make to avoid ultimate collapse are identical to the changes we must make to create the world of our common dream." (3)

It is the ultimate irony that our belief in the survival of the fittest, if held much longer, would actually cause our demise as a species. We are learning instead that our survival depends, not on conquest, but on comprehending the oneness and sacredness of all life.

Not long ago, a whale was caught in a net in San Francisco Bay and surely would have drowned without help. Divers rushed to her side to cut her free, knowing that she could kill any one of them with a thrust of her tail. Yet she patiently waited, being careful not to harm them. When they were finished, instead of swimming away immediately, she took the time to circle the group of divers. Gently and deliberately, she made eye contact with each one. There was a profound connection made that day from whale to humans—gratitude, love, trust—unspoken but deeply known.

New stories emerge daily on YouTube, in books, and in the media telling of animals who are connecting with us, rescuing us, warning us, escaping from the slaughterhouse and crying in some universal language that we all understand—"I want to live!" A tortoise has adopted an orphaned hippopotamus; dogs have healed prison inmates and given comfort to the sick in hospitals. Dolphins have rescued thousands of people. Most recently they were in the news for rescuing a surfer who was in the jaws of a great white shark in Monterey Bay off the coast of California.

Animals are indeed helping us to find peace. Several years ago Ann Wilson rescued two cows from certain death in a slaughterhouse. Now they will live out their lives as part of her family. Ann wrote recently of the gift of peace she has received from them. "What an amazing day it was for me last fall…I lucked out and was able to sit with my two precious moos—Jay & Buddy—on a beautiful Sunday morning while they chewed their cud. I sat there beside both of them in the barn gently stroking their heads and watching as their eyes closed in total relaxation and trust. As I continued to pet their beautiful faces and listened to my cows gently breathe, I realized there was no suffering, no misery at that moment, only peace. I had always wondered what absolute peace would feel like, and if I would *ever* get to experience it in my lifetime. And today, I did. Something so precious and rare…a feeling I will never forget. Thank you Jay & Buddy. You are my peace in this world."

Similarly, Rita Reynolds also rescued a cow whom she named Christina. In Rita's lovely book *Ask the Cow*, she describes the healing she received from this special friendship. One particular day Rita was feeling emotionally and physically drained. She decided to get some fresh air and ended up sitting next to Christina who was napping in the hay. "As I leaned against her," Rita wrote, "I was surprised to find that I began to feel strong and sure of my direction in life again, able to deal with (well, nearly) anything. In those first moments of deeper connection between us, Christina became my anchor to peace..." (4)

We, like Rita and Ann, have one foot in the old world and one in the new. It can be discouraging and stressful to live in these chaotic and violent times. Yet it is essential that we remain positive if we are to have a chance at finding inner peace and creating a culture of peace.

How do we cross this bridge and truly live our common dream? Simply this—we must remember who we are. We are sacred beings, capable of infinite goodness and love. We are born radiating sweetness and tenderness. The miraculous nature that we sense in all babies from the tiniest of frogs and baby birds to human infants is still in each one of us. As Will Tuttle explains it, "As consciousness, we are eternal, free, and benevolent." (5)

Many awakened individuals have predicted this time in our evolution when we would realize who we are. Teilhard de Chardin explained that we would see the beginnings of this massive cosmic awakening around the end of the twentieth century, saying, "The field of mind will awaken and we will rebuild the earth. Remain always true to yourself, but move ever upward toward greater consciousness and greater Love. At the summit, you will find yourself united with all those who from every direction, every culture, have made the same ascent."

It is time. We are capable of allowing divine intelligence and unconditional love to express itself through us. The missing peace has been found. We can put this puzzle together by living our truth and by holding a vision in our minds and hearts of a glorious new earth home where all the water and air is pure and clean; the soil is fertile and uncontaminated; all animals are free; and all of us are vegan, peaceful, nonviolent, and living from our true spiritual nature.

Together, may we hold in our hearts this Buddhist Prayer of Lovingkindness:

> May all beings be peaceful.
> May all beings be happy. May all beings be safe.
> May all beings awaken to the light of their true nature.
> May all beings be free.

# Frequently Asked Questions

*It's a matter of taking the side of the weak against the strong,
something the best people have always done.*
Harriet Beecher Stowe

*As a mother watches over her child,
willing to risk her own life
to protect her only child, so with a boundless heart
should one cherish all living beings, suffusing
the whole world with unobstructed lovingkindness.*
Metta Sutta

As we were putting together this book, we thought some of the questions below might arise for some of our readers. Of course, these questions do not address every aspect of animal liberation or health. There are resources for more information in our "Helpful Sources" section.

**1. The number one question asked by people who still consume animals and their products seems to be: "Where do you get your protein?"**

Since going vegan I've (Tina) been asked the question many times, "Where do you get your protein if you don't eat meat or dairy products?" Believe it or not, vegans get their protein the same way some of the largest herbivores get theirs—from plant foods. Except in cases of extreme undernourishment and starvation, protein deficiency is virtually nonexistent. It is far more likely that ill health will be caused by excessive animal protein consumption. This is the driving force behind the many Western diseases previously mentioned.

Protein is as easy to get as eating a slice of whole wheat bread, which comes without the saturated fats and cholesterol present in animal-derived foods that are so damaging to our health. Ounce for ounce, spinach has more protein than beef. [1]

Here is a partial list of other plants high in protein: legumes (peas, beans, lentils, soy products); grains (wheat, oats, rice, barley, buckwheat, millet); nuts (brazils, hazels, almonds, cashews); seeds (sunflower, pumpkin, sesame); and vegetables.

In short, studies show that vegan diets provide the ideal amounts of protein recommended by the World Health Organization and by the UK's Department of Health. On the other hand, many omnivores eat more protein than guidelines recommend and this may have disadvantages for their health.

[1] *Veggie List Source: Nutritive Value of American Foods in Common Units*, USDA Handbook No. 456.

**2. If we don't eat animals, then we have to eat plants. Doesn't that involve harm, killing and cruelty to the plants?**

When we make the commitment to live an ahimsa or vegan life, we are promising to do the least possible harm. Of course, the ideal is no harm, but in this world as it is today, that is nearly impossible. Fruitarians, who eat only fruit, recognize that the tree from which their food falls actually needs animals to eat the fruit in order to spread its seeds. In this way no harm has been done, and a miraculous cycle of life has been facilitated. Likewise, when we eat from plants such as chard and lettuce, the plant continues to live and produce more leaves. Perennial plants, as well, continue to live after we have eaten parts of them.

However there are plants that we do indeed kill, such as a carrot. Yet as we strive to live by doing the least harm, we can certainly agree that eating a carrot is not the same as eating an animal. Carrots have no central nervous system and, as far as we know, no pain receptors. They do not fight and struggle and scream to stay alive as animals do. Also, because it takes much less land to grow plants to feed people than it does to grow animals to feed the same number of people, we are potentially making more land available for wilderness and eliminating the pollution caused by animal agriculture.

In addition, because animals eat plants as well as feed made of fish and other animals, then we have caused the deaths of thousands more plants and animals and caused more harm than we would have if we had just eaten the plants directly. For example, it takes between fifteen to twenty-five pounds of vegetation to produce one pound of cow meat. Obviously, by eating plants directly we are eating far fewer plants than if we eat food derived from animal sources.

Nevertheless, it is feasible that plants have some sort of awareness. We only need to stand beneath an old tree for a few minutes to feel the possibility of that deep in our souls. Many people who have house plants sense an energy field of peace that emanates from them. There is also a certain joy at the sight of a blooming lotus or the scent of a rose or lilac blossom.

As we stand in awe at the mystery of all life and hold in our hearts a sincere desire to do the least possible harm, we will find our way.

### 3. What do you do about the anger you feel when you see all the horrible things people do to animals?

This is a very real challenge for everyone who begins to bear witness to animal cruelty. It is no wonder that so many people remain purposefully ignorant of this ongoing crisis. Everyone is aware on some unconscious level that the cruelty of human beings to animals is gruesome and nearly unbearable to accept. Most people, when asked, will say they can watch a movie that involves violence among people, but they cannot bear to watch a movie that shows animals suffering.

Nevertheless, some of us do ultimately take the leap into the painful and largely hidden world of animal exploitation. Once we do, we become witnesses, and bearing witness brings with it the responsibility and the desire to do something.

Truly, anger is a stage that most, if not all, people experience at the beginning of this awakened awareness. It can be difficult and painful as we mourn the deaths, face our own complicity, and understand the massive and ongoing extent of the suffering. Most often the anger gets directed at the corporate executives who are behind the scenes of the pollution, human rights violations, and animal cruelty.

This anger can be helpful or destructive, depending on how we utilize it. It is possible to burn out from the fire of the anger and end up feeling alone, cynical or helpless to make a difference. But it is also possible to use the anger to fuel our inner fire. That fire leads us to our own particular right action, whatever it is we are meant to do. And that right action leads to a sense of deep and fulfilling purpose.

Something as simple as picking up a caterpillar from the road so he or she will not be crushed becomes a source of tremendous joy and connection. As we settle into this life of ahimsa, we find ourselves becoming more and more compassionate. Insects whom we may have once seen as pests become fascinating neighbors. We find ourselves learning every day more ways to be kind, and the joy of that is boundless. As this joy grows, we no longer react in an unconscious way. As conscious beings, we become able to transmute anger into energy for the liberation of all beings, but it does take time, and we need to be patient with ourselves.

### 4. Where do we draw the line? What about horseback riding, training dogs, etc.?

A life of nonviolence leads to many insights, but these usually develop over the course of many years. We might start out being vegetarian, and then eliminate dairy and eggs. Soon after, we might discover cruelty-free products and buy only soap that is not tested on animals. As awareness continues to dawn, we may feel compelled to get all the leather and wool out of the house. It takes time, as we find ourselves questioning, one by one, our culturally programmed thoughts and actions. A horse lover who becomes vegan might tune into her horse one day and discover the horse doesn't want to be ridden and never did. Or perhaps, she will find that the horse does enjoy being ridden, but only by certain people, and without a bit in her mouth.

The line, we find, is constantly moving out farther and farther as we grow in consciousness and in sensitivity to the needs, desires, and rights of our animal friends and family members.

### 5. Should animals have rights?

Animals should have the right to equal consideration of their interests. For instance, a dog most certainly has an interest in not having pain inflicted on him or her.

We are human animals, and we share the earth with the other animals. What if a higher being from another planet came to earth and thought us the lesser being? Would our interests still matter to us? Of course they would. We do not have the right to decide who is or is not more important and whose lives mean less. That the lives of animals have their own meaning and value to each one of them is the essential consideration.

When given the choice, it makes sense to choose compassion. This is the core of human ethics—that we have compassion and respect for all others who share our world.

### 6. Dairy products have been stated to be the best source of calcium. Being vegan would leave humans open to calcium deficiencies, right?

The Physicians Committee for Responsible Medicine (pcrm.org) states that, "Diets that are high in protein cause more calcium to be lost through the urine. Protein from animal products is much more likely to cause calcium loss than protein from plant foods. This may be one reason that vegetarians tend to have stronger bones than meat-eaters."

A quick list of foods that contain significant amounts of calcium includes: broccoli, brussel sprouts, butternut squash, beans, carrots, cauliflower, collards, kale, sweet potato, sesame seeds, beans of all kinds, soymilk, tofu, tortillas, whole wheat bread, whole wheat flour, rice milk, dried figs, oranges, and raisins. Dairy products are not needed and can do more harm than good.

### 7. If using animals is unethical, why does the Bible say that we have dominion over animals?

Dominion is not the same as tyranny. Parents have dominion over their children, but that doesn't mean that they can eat them, wear them, or experiment on them. If we have dominion over animals, surely it is to protect them, not to use them for our own ends. There is nothing in the Bible that would justify our modern-day practices, which desecrate the environment, destroy entire species of wildlife, and inflict torment and death on billions of animals every year. The Bible imparts a reverence for life, and a loving God could not help but be appalled by the way that animals are treated today.

### 8. What about hunting? I've heard that it helps conservation of wildlife by thinning out the herds so there will be plenty to eat and wildlife won't starve to death.

The conservation argument presented by hunters seems to imply that hunting actually helps animals and is, therefore, an act of kindness, not violence. The basic assertion is that there are too many of a certain animal, and, therefore, they will die slowly of starvation, so hunters will do them a favor by killing them quickly.

There are several reasons why this is not logical. When there is a shortage of food, it is the elderly, sick, and young animals who may starve. Yet hunters target the healthiest and most beautiful animals for meat and trophies. Also, there may be other animals such as skunks and mice who may be at risk of starvation, but they are not targeted.

Game conservation policies include the killing of predators, clear cutting of forests, and the planting of forage, among other practices, in order to increase the populations of "game" animals. This severely alters the ecological balance. In addition, many animals, especially birds, are raised in captivity and released during hunting season so that they can be shot. Many hunters pay to kill animals at canned hunts, which are areas in which the animals are enclosed by fences and cannot escape certain death.

Of course, not every shot kills immediately. Many animals are left to suffer and die from gunshot and arrow wounds. Many others are severely traumatized by the loss of loved ones and the terror that they must endure during hunting seasons.

The bottom line is that, as we have stated throughout this book, we are not here to cause suffering and death to the animals with whom we share this earth.

# Helpful Sources

**Books**

*America Fooled*, Dr. Timothy Scott
*Animal Gospel*, Andrew Linzey
*Animal Rites*, Andrew Linzey
*Animal Theology*, Andrew Linzey
*Animals as Persons*, Gary L. Francione
*Appetite for Profit*, Michele Simon
*Becoming Vegan*, Brenda Davis and Vesanto Melina
*Bird Flu*, Dr. Michael Greger
*The Case for Animal Rights*, Tom Regan
*The China Study*, T. Colin Campbell
*Diet for a New America*, John Robbins
*Dominion*, Matthew Scully
*The Dominion of Love*, Norm Phelps
*Dying for a Hamburger*, Murray Waldman, M.D. and Marjorie Lamb
*Eat Here*, Brian Halweil
*Eat Right, Live Longer*, Neal D. Barnard, M.D.
*Eat to Live*, Dr. Joel Fuhrman
*The Emotional Lives of Animals*, Marc Bekoff
*Famous Vegetarians*, Rynn Berry
*Fast Food Craze*, Tina Volpe
*Food for Life*, Neal D. Barnard, M.D.
*The Food Revolution*, John Robbins
*Good News for All Creation*, Stephen Kaufman
*The Holocaust and the Henmaid's Tale*, Karen Davis, Ph.D.
*The Longest Struggle*, Norm Phelps
*The Lost Religion of Jesus*, Keith Akers
*Mad Cowboy*, Howard Lyman

*Mad Sheep*, Linda Fallace
*The McDougall Plan*, John A. McDougall, M.D.
*The Pig Who Sang to the Moon*, Jeffrey Masson
*Peace to All Beings*, Judy Carman
*The Power of Your Plate*, Neal D. Barnard, M.D.
*Prevent and Reverse Heart Disease*, Caldwell Esselstyn, Jr., M.D.
*Rattling the Cage*, Steven M. Wise
*The Rave Diet & Lifestyle*, Mike Anderson
*Seal Wars*, Captain Paul Watson
*The Sexual Politics of Meat*, Carol Adams
*Skinny Bitch*, Rory Freedman and Kim Barnouin
*Slaughterhouse*, Gail Eiznitz
*An Unnatural Order*, Jim Mason
*Vegetarian America*, Karen and Michael Iacobbo
*Vegetarians and Vegans in America Today*, Karen and Michael Iacobbo

## Websites

All Creatures Ministry, allcreatures.org
Animal Acres, animalacres.org
Christian Vegetarian Association, christianveg.com
Compassionate Spirit, compassionatespirit.com
DawnWatch, dawnwatch.com
Dr. McDougall's Right Foods, rightfoods.com
Earthsave International, earthsave.org
Farm Sanctuary, farmsanctuary.org
Friends of Animals, friendsofanimals.org
Humane Myth, humanemyth.org
Humane Society of the U.S., hsus.org
In Defense of Animals, idausa.org
International Vegetarian Union, ivu.org
Kinship Circle, kinshipcircle.org
Nonviolence United, nonviolenceunited.org
Physicians Committee for Responsible Medicine, pcrm.org
People for the Ethical Treatment of Animals, peta.org
Sea Shepherd Society, seashepherd.org

Society of Religious and Ethical Vegetarians, serv-online.org
Tribe of Heart, tribeofheart.org
United Poultry Concerns, upc-online.org
Vegan Outreach, veganoutreach.org
Veg Dining, vegdining.com
Vegetarian Resources, goveg.com
*Wake Up America* Radio Show, modavox.com
Worldwide Prayer Circle for Animals, circleofcompassion.org

# ENDNOTES

**Introduction to Part I**

1. Bennett, Denise. *The Enlightened Path of Health...An Intentional Journey.* Sedona, AZ: Light the Way Publishing, 2006, p. xi.
2. Towns, Sharon and David, Ed. *Voices from the Garden: Stories of Becoming a Vegetarian.* New York: Lantern Books, 2001, p. 81.
3. Ibid., p. 85.
4. Ibid., p. 114.

**Chapter Three**
"Becoming as a Little Child"

1. Matthew 18:1,3 (King James Version).
2. *Science and Health with Key to the Scriptures* by Mary Baker Eddy, pp. 323-324 (within the citation is Matthew 5:8).
3. *Miscellaneous Writings 1883-1896* by Mary Baker Eddy, p. 36.
4. *Science and Health*, p. 374.
5. *The Christian Science Journal*, September 2007, Vol. 125, No. 09, "An Ever-Rising Career Arc" by Keith S. Collins, pp. 42-43.

**Chapter Four**
Introduction

1. Berry, Rynn. *Famous Vegetarians and Their Favorite Recipes: Lives and Lore from Buddha to the Beatles.* New York: Pythagorean Publishers, 2003.
2. Emerson, Marjorie. Online Quaker newsletter, "The Peaceable Table", 7-04, vegetarianfriends.net.

**Chapter Twelve**
Tina's Story

1. Linzey, Andrew, *Animal Gospel.* Louisville, Ky: Westminster John Knox Press, p. 22.

## Chapter Thirteen

1. Yogananda, Paramahansa. *The Divine Romance.* Los Angeles, CA: Self Realization Fellowship, 1986, p. 452.

2. Cousens, Gabriel. *Conscious Eating.* Santa Rosa , CA: Vision Books International, 1992, p. 246.

3. International Vegetarian Union, ivu.org.

4. Riedweg, Christoph. *Pythagoras: His Life, Teaching and Influence.* Cornell University, 2005, pp. 5–6, 59, 73.

5. Aristotle, *Metaphysics 1-5,* cc. 350 BC; Books I-IX (Loeb Classical Library).

6. Ayto, John; Ian Crofton. *Brewer's Dictionary of Phrase and Fable, Second Edition.* London: Weidenfeld & Nicholson, 2006, p. 870.

7. Collinson, Diane, *Fifty Major Philosophers,* New York, NY: Routledge, 1997, p. 9.

8. Berry, Rynn. *Famous Vegetarians & Their Favorite Recipes: Lives and Lore from Buddha to the Beatles.* New York: Pythagorean Publishers, 2003.

9. Ibid.

10. SERV (Society of Ethical and Religious Vegetarians) Writing committee, "Vegetarianism and the Major World Religions", serv-on-line.org/pamphlet2005. See also Akers, Keith. *A Vegetarian Sourcebook: The Nutrition Ecology and Ethics of a Natural Foods Diet.* Denver, CO: Vegetarian Press, 1993, p. 181.

11. Ibid.

12. For detailed treatises on this subject, see Will Tuttle's *World Peace Diet* and Jim Mason's *An Unnatural Order.*

13. Berry, op. cit.

14. Berry, op. cit.

15. Phelps, Norm. *The Dominion of Love: Animal Rights According to the Bible,* New York, NY: Lantern Books, 2002.

16. Ibid.

17. Akers, Keith, *The Lost Religion of Jesus: Simple Living and Nonviolence in Early Christianity.* New York, NY: Lantern Books, 2000, p. 134.

18. Ibid., p. 25

19. Linzey, Andrew. *Animal Rites: Liturgies of Animal Care*. London: SCM Press, 1999.

20. Berry, op. cit.

21. Ellwood, Gracia Fay, Editor. Online Quaker newsletter, "The Peaceable Table," 2-07. vegetarianfriends.net.

22. Vezzosi, Alessandro, *Leonardo da Vinci: Renaissance Man*. London: Thames & Hudson, New Horizons, 1997.

23. Vasari, Giorgio. *Lives of the Artists*, 1568; Penguin Classics, trans. George Bull 1965.

24. Roberts, Holly. *Vegetarian Christian Saints: Mystics, Ascetics, and Monks*. San Francisco, CA: Anjeli Press, 2004, p. 193.

25. Ibid.

26. Ibid.

27. Ellwood, op. cit., Jan., 06.

## Chapter Fourteen

1. Fillmore, Charles. "The Vegetarian", May, 1920.

2. Fillmore, Charles. "Flesh-Eating Metaphysically Considered", May, 1910.

3. Gandhi, Mahatma. *An Autobiography: The Story of My Experiences with Truth*. Boston: Beacon Press, 1957.

4. Ibid.

5. Ibid.

6. www.nonresistance.org.

7. www.online-literature.com/tolstoy/2733/.

8. Gold, Gerald and Richard Attenborough. *Gandhi: A Pictorial Biography*. New York, NY: Newmarket Press, 1983.

9. Gandhi, Mahatma. "Mahatma Gandhi and Leo Tolstoy Letters". Long Beach, CA: Long Beach Publications, September, 1987.

10. Tolstoy, Leo. "The First Step", translated by Aylmer Maude in *Essays and Letters*. New York: H. Frowde, 1909, pp. 82–91.

11. Ibid.

12. "Livestock's Long Shadow: Environmental Issues and Options" is a United Nations report, released by the Food and Agriculture Organization of the U.N. on November 29, 2006.

13. "Fight Global Warming by Going Vegetarian" is an article from www.goveg.com.

14. Hanh, Thich Nhat. "Letter from Thay", posted 10.12.2007 on plumvillage.org.

15. Speech by the Dalai Lama, cited on rawveg.info/buddhistvegetarian.

16. NobelPrize.org.

17. www.time.com/time/time100.

18. Einstein, Albert. *Ideas and Opinions*. New York: Wings Books, 1954.

19. Translation of letter to Hermann Huth, December 27, 1930. Einstein Archive 46–756.

20. United Nations radio interview recorded in Einstein's study, Princeton, New Jersey, 1950 wikiquote.com.

21. Dear, Father John. *Christianity and Vegetarianism: Pursuing the Nonviolence of Jesus*. Booklet printed by People for the Ethical Treatment of Animals, Norfolk, VA.

22. Dear, Father John. "The only diet for a peacemaker is a vegetarian diet". Posted on ncrcafe.org on July-8-08. Also see www.fatherjohndear.org.

23. *Unitarian Universalist World* journal, Summer, 2008 issue.

24. "Mercy and Kindness: An Islamic imam shares his view of respect for animals", *Best Friends Magazine*, Nov/Dec, 2007, p. 3.

25. Schwartz, Richard. *Judaism and Vegetarianism*. New York, NY: Lantern Books, 2001, pp. 180-181.

26. *American Vegan: Ahimsa Lights the Way Magazine*. Summer, 2008 issue, pp. 12–13.

**Chapter Fifteen**

1. Tietz, Jeff. "Boss Hog", *Rolling Stone*, December 2006.

**Chapter Sixteen**

1. Tuttle, Will. *The World Peace Diet: Eating for Spiritual Health and Social Harmony*. New York: Lantern Books, 2005.

2. Berry, Wendell. *The Long Legged House*. New York: Harcourt, Brace, Jovanovich, 1972.

3. Korten, David. "We are hard-wired to care and connect", *Yes!: Building a Just and Sustainable World*, Issue 67, Fall, 2008.

4. Reynolds, Rita M. *Ask the Cow: A Gentle Guide to Finding Peace.* Exeter, NH: Publishing Works, Inc. 2008, p. 15.

5. Tuttle, op. cit.

# ABOUT THE AUTHORS

**Tina**

Tina Volpe was raised in Lake View Terrace, California, a northern horsy suburb of Los Angeles. As a child, Volpe's home included many farm animals, most of whom were eventually slaughtered for food for the family. Volpe endured many serious emotional blows from seeing family friends (pigs, cows) being slaughtered and hung up from trees. This had a lifetime effect on her.

As a result of her love for, and interaction with animals, Volpe became a vegetarian over three decades ago. Over the past eight years, she has been studying the farm industry and the effects its business decisions and resulting procedures have on animals. This research convinced her that while animal rights groups have made advances in informing the public about farm industry carelessness, more efforts are needed because animals are still suffering at the hand of agribusiness.

Tina Volpe is the author of the book *The Fast Food Craze: Wreaking Havoc on Our Bodies and Our Animals*. She is a health researcher, speaker, educator, consultant, columnist, and television guest. She previously hosted the top-rated radio show *Wake Up America* on Global Talk Radio. Her weekly show of the same title can now be heard at Voice America Radio. Tina is affiliated with the Physicians Committee for Responsible Medicine as a "Heart Health" speaker, and with SPEAK (Supporting and Promoting Ethics for the Animal Kingdom) as a Humane Educator. She lives on a ranch in Northern Arizona with her family and 21 unique animal friends.

**Judy**

Judy Carman, M.A. is a former counselor and program director for mental health clinics. As an author and activist for animal rights, environmental protection, and world peace, she has helped establish organizations both for adults and children over the years. Most recently she has co-founded Animal Outreach of Kansas (animaloutreach-ks.org) and the Worldwide Prayer Circle for Animals (circleofcompassion.org) and is also a Peace Representative of the World Peace Prayer Society (worldpeace.org). She is part of an animal rescue network and has been deployed to several disaster areas to help animals and their people.

Her books include *Born to Be Blessed: Seven Keys to Joyful Living* and *Peace to All Beings: Veggie Soup for the Chicken's Soul.* Her *Peace to All Beings* was judged one of the best spiritual books of 2003. In it Judy introduced the concept of *Homo ahimsa* (ahimsa is the Sanskrit word for nonviolence and lovingkindness) to describe the new compassionate human that we will become if enough of humanity awakens in time.

Judy is featured in *Vegetarians and Vegans in America Today* by Karen and Michael Iacobbo and contributes articles and essays to newspapers, books, and magazines. Some of her articles can be found at circleofcompassion.org, along with excerpts from *Peace to all Beings.* She has been a keynote speaker and workshop leader at many conferences.

Having once lived off the utility grid in a tipi, Judy and her husband Michael, both vegan, now live in an almost totally solar-heated home in Kansas, with plans for solar and wind powered electricity. Their vehicles run on used veggie oil. They have three adult children and six grandchildren.

Please visit Judy's Prayer Circle for Animals (co-founded with Will and Madeleine Tuttle at circleofcompassion.org) to read about the prayer being spoken around the world for the animals. You can register your name and location on the world map if you would like to be part of this worldwide prayer circle. The prayer that each member of the circle repeats each day is:

*Compassion Encircles the Earth*
*for All Beings Everywhere*